P9-BZG-454

10
Excellent Reasons
Not to Hate Taxes

Introduction by David Cay Johnston

Edited by Stephanie Greenwood

THE NEW PRESS

NEW YORK
LONDON

Requests for permission to reproduce selections from this book should be mailed to: Permissions Department, The New Press, 38 Greene Street, New York, NY 10013.

Published in the United States by The New Press, New York, 2007
Distributed by W. W. Norton & Company, Inc., New York

LIBRARY OF CONGRESS CATALOGING-IN-PUBLICATION DATA

10 excellent reasons not to hate taxes / introduction by David Cay Johnston; edited by Stephanie Greenwood.
p. cm.
Includes bibliographical references.
ISBN 978-1-59558-161-7 (pbk.)
1. Taxation—United States.   2. Income tax—United States.   3. Democracy—United States.   I. Greenwood, Stephanie.   II. Title: Ten excellent reasons not to hate taxes.

HJ2381.A6 2007
336.200973—dc22   2007021462

The New Press was established in 1990 as a not-for-profit alternative to the large, commercial publishing houses currently dominating the book publishing industry. The New Press operates in the public interest rather than for private gain, and is committed to publishing, in innovative ways, works of educational, cultural, and community value that are often deemed insufficiently profitable.

www.thenewpress.com

Composition by Westchester Book Group

Printed in Canada

2   4   6   8   10   9   7   5   3   1

Contents

Introduction

Don't you just hate paying taxes? All that work and along comes the government to take a chunk of your money. And for what?

Now *that* is the right question, the one so often ignored. Just what do our taxes buy us?

For starters, taxes buy us freedom. They buy us civilization. They buy us prosperity. They finance America.

It is easy to think that the benefits of living in America are just there for the taking, like the morning sun and the air. This shallow belief gains currency when an entire generation of Americans has heard from their political leaders one overwhelming message—elect me, and I will cut your taxes.

Hardly anyone has the courage these days to tell you that paying taxes, like eating spinach, is good for you. Or that a diet of tax cuts financed with borrowed money will leave society weakened and burdened with debt.

The perception that taxes are pure waste is reinforced by the superficial way that many news organizations cover the issue, especially the implicit assumption that taxes are bad, and anything called a tax cut is good. Thoughtless coverage tends to drown out thoughtful ideas.

The sixteen writers whose work fills these pages know better. They understand that, as chapter 10 points out, Justice Oliver Wendell Holmes' 1927 observation still holds: "taxes are what we pay for a civilized society."

The writers of these essays all provide thoughtful, sometimes provocative ideas, about the central role that taxes play in a democratic society. No one will agree with everything they wrote—I certainly do not.

The value of their words, however, is insights—many drawn from classic wisdom passed down through the ages—that give substance to the rationale for taxes and that show a well-designed system to raise and spend public funds not only can maintain society, but can make us all richer in wallet and in spirit.

Like all valuable writing, these essays invite us to ponder whether what we imagine to be actually is. They urge us to reconsider our societal assumptions, and they offer us a grammar of tax so that we can better understand the issues.

These writers also understand that freedom is not free. Our freedoms are the product of thousands of years of struggle, often violent, as well as the intensive development of the philosophical basis for self-governance. Taxes have played a central, and little appreciated, role in that struggle, beginning more than two millennia ago in Athens when a change in the tax system gave us both a moral basis for imposing taxes and the first democracy.

Three of these essays examine the moral component of taxes. In chapter 1 Matthew Gardner of the Institute on Taxation and Economic Policy explains the rationale for progressive taxes. In chapter 10 Miles Rapoport, Michael Lipsky, and Stuart Comstock-Gay of Dēmos, a network promoting democratic participation, and Stephanie Greenwood, the editor of this book, show that starving the tax system starves our democracy.

Susan Pace Hamill, a professor of law at the University of Alabama who also holds a divinity degree, argues persuasively that our tax system today violates basic Judeo-Christian ethics, to which the vast majority of Americans say they subscribe. "The discussion surrounding tax policy at the highest federal levels," she writes in a thoughtful jeremiad, "exalts private property rights above all other concerns, reflecting the values of objectivist ethics, a form of atheism that worships the individual."

Beyond the sin of greed, Professor Hamill reminds, is a religious obligation to sacrifice for the poor. But our society, she shows, behaves as if camels pass easily through the eyes of needles and that the rich will be welcomed into the kingdom of God, contrary to what the Bible says.

We live in the not yet finished era of rule by those who, through brute force or claims of divine right, set themselves up as warlords, kings, pharaohs, prophets, czars, supreme leaders, or any of the titles that convey dictatorial power. First the nobles and then the burghers demanded a share of power—and a role in taxation. And in 1776 Thomas Jefferson articulated the radical idea that all men are created equal, an ideal we have yet to perfect.

Americans, however, know little of the role of taxes in this struggle, and much of what they do know is false.

Few know that the Rosetta stone, which allowed us to translate Egyptian hieroglyphics, is a grant of tax relief. The terms of that relief remind us, as the Old Preacher says in *Ecclesiastes*, that there is nothing new under the sun. The relief was given to those who ensured the fealty of the people to the pharaoh.

Ask almost any American about the Boston Tea Party, and they will tell you that it was a protest against high taxes. It was not. The idea that the colonies were overtaxed is laughable since per capita taxes in the mother country were fifty times those in the colonies.

The thousands who gathered in the rain outside Old South Church on December 16, 1773, came to protest a tax favor granted to the friends of King George III. These friends had been granted a royal monopoly, which at the time was the biggest commercial enterprise in the world, the British East India Company. To stave off bankruptcy caused by mismanagement, they received a tax exemption on a surfeit of tea. In the colonies this tax exemption was a threat to every petty merchant who sold tea and to every customer because it would result in higher prices and an end to competition.

Even today tax favors, as well as tax rates, give rise to popular discontent. And yet as a people we seem far less sophisticated about these issues and certainly less willing to endure any discomfort to learn the hard truths about them.

Just a few years after the Boston Tea Party, after our mostly guerilla tactics defeated the Red Coats, the first American experiment in self-government failed. Under the Articles of Confederation, the central government had no effective power to tax, and so it collapsed.

Americans had not learned a basic lesson, one that the British philosopher Edmund Burke wrote in his famous 1793 letter that began the modern conservative movement: *the revenue of the state is the state.*[1]

In writing our Constitution, which in its preamble says we established our union to promote the general welfare, the framers put taxes first among the powers that we grant our lawmakers: "The Congress shall have the power to lay and collect taxes, duties and imposts," is language as broad as it is sparse. Those fourteen words establish that Congress can tax almost anything and, thus, make the form and burden of taxation a political issue that will last as long as our Republic survives.

The test of a tax system is whether it serves the economic and social order or cuts against it. David Ricardo, one of the first economists, outlined four principles of a tax system that endures. Taxes should be transparent; simple; place roughly equal burdens on people of similar situations, known as "horizontal equity"; and should be based on ability to pay, known as "vertical progressivity." Our system today is none of these.

That last principle is part of the very idea that gave us democracy. When ancient Athens was ruled by dictators, an era we now call the tyranny, each person paid the same tax. This levy was an onerous burden for nearly all except the rich. Thinking about this tax burden eventually gave birth to the moral basis of tax—the more an individual gains from living in a civilized society, the greater his obligation to maintain that society with his taxes.

We have largely forgotten this principle in America, which today has a tax system that takes from those with less to lavish favors on the rich. As Warren Buffett has observed, he pays a much smaller tax on his last dollar of income than his secretary pays on her last dollar.

A world without taxes is a world of raw nature, where only the fittest survive. There is no wealth without taxes for there is no civil order. That home you worked so hard to possess is yours only because the law says so. If some gang of thieves tries to take it from you, the government will protect your interest. The taxpayer-financed system of civil justice also diminishes violent disputes. But rights without the ability to protect and enforce them are not rights at all. And without taxes there is no enforcement of rights.

Another important concept that these authors explain is how taxes can make us richer, hardly what most of us imagine. Jeff Madrick of *Challenge Magazine* and Meizhu Lui of the advocacy group United for a Fair Economy show how a well-tuned tax system promotes economic growth. Together, John Abrams of the South Mountain Company, an innovative designer and builder of affordable housing, and Greg LeRoy of the advocacy organization Good Jobs First, show how taxes are actually good for business.

The idea that we are just passing through, stewards of our planet and our society only during our lifetimes is often lost in tax debates. But a society that does not invest heavily in its future cannot endure. Stan Karp and Nancy Folbre, in their respective essays on education and children, show us the crucial role of taxes to America's endurance. Chuck Collins explains the role of taxes in economic renewal, in ensuring that our society provides opportunities for generations to come, lest we become like late eighteenth-century France, where enterprise was irrelevant because the tax and property rules determined everyone's fate at birth.

John Fitzgerald, who has since joined the Society for Conservation Biology, and Daphne Wysham of the Institute for Policy Studies show how changes in our tax system could protect the environment. Their idea shows signs of becoming mainstream; for example, in 2006 *Forbes* magazine proposed a carbon tax to reduce pollution.

While taxes can make us richer, today they are making us poorer. They discourage work, drive investment and jobs offshore, and increasingly distribute the burden on those with modest economic benefits from living in our society.

Poverty is on the rise in America, despite our growing abundance. But inadequate incomes are only one kind of poverty. Growing even faster is a poverty of ideas about how to sustain our society and create a more perfect union that promotes the general welfare, the very reason for our Constitution.

Although slim in size, this volume is so fat with ideas that it can nurture many years of thought after you lay these pages down. To be free, and to be free to prosper, we need to keep in mind, as the authors of these essays do, that while the power to tax is the power to destroy, it is also the power to create a free, prosperous, and healthy society. Taxation is the fount of liberty.

Let us remember that without taxes there is no America. Let us remember the most conservative of principles, that those who gain the most from a society have a moral duty to bear the greatest burden of maintaining that society.

We need a tax system designed to grease the wheels of economic growth, reward good behavior, encourage prosperity, succor the poor and give them the tools to succeed, educate new generations of Americans, and perpetuate what we have built, not just in the physical world, but in the realm of ideals.

Without a principled tax system America will wither. Let us do our best to ensure the day never comes when, as with the first American government, our tax system destroys what we have. Let us work to ensure as best we can that students will never read a history text that begins with the words "The United States of America was . . ."

David Cay Johnston
Rochester, New York
April 2007

1

Progressive taxes are a good deal
The Fundamentals of Our Federal Tax System

Matthew Gardner

The federal tax system has been at the heart of a political firestorm for almost a decade. Basic questions about the level and distribution of federal taxes have been debated fiercely, with some arguing that taxes are mainly a drag on productive society and should be reduced as much as possible and others insisting on the importance of maintaining tax revenues to fund programs or control the deficit. These questions are fundamental to the workings of our government: taxes fund public services, and to the extent that we want the latter, we have to put up with the former.

But debate about how to balance public services and taxes has been short-circuited by a series of tax cuts pushed through Congress by Republican leaders and signed by President Bush beginning in 2001. Unable to gain support for direct cuts in spending, they instead used technical rule-making procedures and their slim majority

Matthew Gardner is the state tax policy director for the Institute on Taxation and Economic Policy.

control to pass budgets that forced a dramatic scaling-back of public investments by "starving the beast."

Understanding the basics of the federal tax system, and the impact of the Bush tax cuts on this system, will be crucial in the coming years to revive a healthy democratic debate about the size and quality and very role of national government.

How High Are U.S. Taxes Compared with Those of Other Developed Nations?

For all the anti-tax posturing we hear every day, one would think that U.S. taxes are unusually high. But a comparison with other industrialized countries shows just the opposite: in the Organization for Economic Cooperation and Development's (OECD) annual survey of thirty countries in Europe, North America, and Asia, as of 2007, the United States ranked twenty-ninth in national and local taxes as a share of Gross Domestic Product (GDP).[1] In 2003, taxes in the thirty countries ranged from a high of 50.8 percent of GDP in Sweden to a low of 19.5 percent in Mexico. Total U.S. taxes (including federal, state, and local) were 24.2 percent of GDP—well below the thirty-country average of 36.5 percent.

Not surprisingly, U.S. residents get what they pay for: our relatively low tax levels yield sub-par public services compared with those of other developed nations. Health insurance and higher education stand out as services that are commonly provided by governments in other countries to a greater degree than in the United States.

Of course, tax rankings as a share of GDP don't tell us much about how people in the United States experience the tax system. U.S. federal taxes are progressive, meaning that well-off people pay a higher share of their income than do middle- and low-income people. The system is made even more progressive through deductions, exemptions and tax credits that disproportionately benefit low- and middle-income households. The progressiveness of our tax system makes the trade-off between taxes and

Breakdown of Federal Revenue by Source

Source of Revenue	Percent of Total Revenue
Personal Income Taxes	43%
Social Security and Medicare Payroll Taxes	37%
Corporate Income Tax	13%
Other Taxes (including estate tax)	7%

Source: Based on figures from the Institute on Taxation and Economic Policy.

public services a beneficial one for most citizens. However, the recent tax cuts and the anti-tax movement behind them threaten to undermine the progressivity that makes the tax system a good deal.

We pay three main types of federal taxes: personal income, payroll, and corporate income. In fiscal year 2005, personal income taxes accounted for the largest share of federal revenues, 43 percent. Social Security and Medicare payroll taxes raised almost 37 percent, and the corporate income tax contributed 13 percent. The remaining 7 percent came from an assortment of other taxes, mostly excise taxes, customs duties, and estate taxes.

The Federal Personal Income Tax

Our federal tax system is progressive mainly thanks to the personal income tax. This is true for a few reasons:

1. *Progressive tax rates increase as income rises.* As mentioned previously, people in lower-income brackets pay a lower rate than people in higher-income brackets. For example, the "marginal" tax rate, or rate charged on the last dollar earned, ranged from 10 percent to 35 percent in 2006. Rate brackets apply to income after a series of progressive deductions and exemptions are taken, so most families pay taxes at the lower rates.

2. *The standard deduction and personal exemptions are worth more to middle- and low-income families than to*

the well-off.[2] Personal exemptions are applied based on family size, not on income. So low-income families can exclude a higher portion of their income than higher-income families of the same size. For example, a family of four can claim $11,200 in personal exemptions. A four-person family making $45,000 would exclude almost a quarter of income. A family of the same size making $112,000 would thus be able to exclude only 10 percent of its income.

3. *Tax credits are targeted to lower- and middle-income families with children.* After the tax rates are applied to taxable income, many taxpayers can use credits to reduce their tax liability further. The single largest credit is the Earned Income Tax Credit (EITC). The EITC is refundable, so families can receive payments above and beyond their federal income tax liability. The second biggest tax credit, also for families with children, equals $1,000 per child, and is generally available to families making up to $100,000.

Because of these progressive features of the income tax, taxpayers in the middle 20 percent pay only 6 percent of their income in personal income taxes. Due to the EITC, the poorest 20 percent actually have a negative tax rate of –3.8 percent. On the other hand, taxpayers in the wealthiest 1 percent of the income scale—those with an average income of $915,000—pay 24.6 percent of their income in federal personal income tax.

Progressivity of Personal Income Tax

	Percent of Income Paid in Personal Income Tax	
	Before credits and deductions	After credits and deductions
Poorest 20 percent	7.9%	−3.8%
Middle 20 percent	15.8%	6.0%
Wealthiest 1 percent	24.6%	24.6%

Source: Based on figures from the Institute on Taxation and Economic Policy.

Although the personal income tax is progressive, it has some very significant loopholes for the well-off. For example, capital gains—income from the sale of stocks and other investments—and dividends are taxed at much lower rates than income from wages. These tax breaks overwhelmingly benefit those with very high incomes, who have most of the capital gains and dividend income. Eliminating tax loopholes such as this and using the resulting revenues to help middle- and low-income families would make the income tax both more progressive and much simpler. But even without such reforms, the overall progressivity of the income tax makes it a good deal for most Americans.

Social Security and Medicare Taxes

The second largest source of federal revenues is payroll taxes, which are used to pay for Social Security and Medicare.[3] Payroll taxes, unlike the personal income tax, are *regressive*, meaning they burden low-income people more than high-income people.

Payroll taxes apply to the very first dollar a person earns. They do not apply to investment income, and a significant portion of the tax is capped, meaning it is only charged on the first portion of earned income up to a threshold amount. Social Security taxes, for example, were calculated as a percentage of wages up to a cap of $94,200 in 2006. Beyond this amount, no tax applies. As a result, payroll taxes take only 2.3 percent of the total income of the wealthiest 1 percent of Americans, who receive most of their income from nonwage sources. That's much lower than the 10.9 percent effective payroll tax rate that the middle 20 percent pays and the 8.1 percent of income paid in payroll taxes by the poorest 20 percent.[4]

Many people find the regressive nature of payroll taxes troubling. Indeed, one reason the Earned Income Tax Credit was adopted was to help offset the payroll taxes of lower-income working people. The structure of the payroll tax is

Regressivity of Payroll Taxes

	Percent of Income Paid in Payroll Taxes
Poorest 20 percent	8.1%
Middle 20 percent	10.9%
Wealthiest 1 percent	2.3%

Source: Based on figures from the Institute on Taxation and Economic Policy.

consistent, however, with Social Security's role as a retirement insurance program. Better-off workers receive somewhat greater retirement benefits under the program, but those added benefits are not in proportion to the taxes they pay into the system. Conversely, lower-income workers receive benefits that are high relative to the taxes they pay into the system.

For most Americans the payroll tax represents the largest single federal tax they pay. In fact, almost three-quarters of all taxpayers pay more in payroll taxes than in federal income taxes. But Social Security and Medicare are the federal government programs from which most Americans derive the greatest benefit.

Corporate Income Tax

The corporate income tax, which is highly progressive, has been a declining source of revenue for many decades. It was cut drastically in the early 1970s and again in the early 1980s. Although corporate income tax revenues revived a bit after reforms in the mid-1980s and early 1990s, its effectiveness has been greatly reduced in the last decade. Multinational corporations have become increasingly aggressive at avoiding taxes, and the corporate Alternative Minimum Tax (AMT), which served for a while to ensure that large, profitable corporations paid at least some federal income tax, has been gutted in recent years.

The corporate income tax lowers the cash income of the wealthiest 1 percent of Americans by 7.8 percent. For the middle 20 percent, the rate is 1.5 percent, and for the poorest 20 percent, it is only 0.9 percent. Reductions in the corporate income tax mean that the system overall becomes less progressive.

The Tax Policy Challenge Posed by the Bush Tax Cuts

The centerpiece of President Bush's tax policy has been dramatic cuts in the most progressive elements of the tax system—personal and corporate income tax—coupled with outright repeal of the federal estate tax, which is the country's most progressive tax. In addition to lowering the *types* of taxes that disproportionately affect the wealthy, the *amount* of tax relief has also been skewed toward those at the top. In 2007, 37 percent of the benefits from the Bush tax cuts went to the very wealthiest 1 percent of the population, while the poorest 20 percent received just over 1 percent of the cuts.

The Bush tax cuts have also spawned a fiscal crisis of historic proportions. The direct cost of the Bush tax cuts between 2001 and 2010 will be approximately $1.85 trillion. Adding the $505 billion in interest on the national debt attributable to the tax cuts over this period, the total cost of the Bush tax cuts will be about $2.36 trillion—almost all of which will be paid for by borrowing. Paring back at least some of the cuts will be an essential step toward restoring fiscal balance.

The Bush tax cuts have also exacerbated an already-growing structural problem in the federal tax system: the federal AMT. Originally designed to ensure that a small group of the wealthiest Americans pays at least some of their income in tax, the AMT now threatens to hit millions of upper-middle-income families. The most obvious AMT fix, increasing the AMT exemptions, would cost nearly a trillion dollars over ten years. A way to pay for this needed change without breaking the bank, however, would be eliminating the special AMT tax break for capital gains and dividends. With a few additional tweaks, this approach could be enacted in a way that wouldn't cost the federal treasury a dime.

The 2001 tax cuts will expire in 2011 unless Congress takes action to extend them. (This ten-year window is thanks to a gimmick in the budget rules used to pass them in the first place.) However, the consequences of leaving the tax cuts until 2011, and certainly of extending them beyond then, would be dire.

The real-world results of "playing chicken" with fiscal policy have proven disastrous in the past: we tried cutting taxes without reducing outlays in the 1980s and ended up adding $3 trillion to the national debt. Fiscally responsible tax increases and spending cuts enacted by the Clinton administration temporarily helped to fill in this fiscal hole, but we're now once again paying the price for unfunded federal tax cuts, with fully 20 percent of the non–Social Security federal budget going to interest payments on the debt.

Adding It All Up

The federal tax system isn't as progressive as it used to be, or as it could be. When all the federal taxes are added up, our tax system remains moderately progressive—mostly because of the personal income tax—even after the damaging effect of the Bush tax cuts. That's only fair, since the people who have the most money have received the greatest benefits from our society and ought to pay more to help support it. But federal taxes are comparatively low and getting lower, and important challenges remain if we are to preserve a fair and adequate tax system in a post-Bush era. Federal policymakers will have plenty of chances, in the next four years and beyond, to take back the ground that has been lost since 2001.

2

They're a moral obligation
Religious and Ethical Arguments for
Progressive Taxation[1]

Susan Pace Hamill

Almost 80 percent of Americans claim to adhere to Christianity or Judaism, but probably few realize that tax policy is one of the most important moral issues we face in the twenty-first century. A tax is a compulsory payment imposed by a government to meet public needs. The Bible directly affirms taxes as legitimate[2] and provides broad standards of justice addressing what tax revenues must cover and how the burden for paying taxes must be spread out.

Judeo-Christian standards of justice require enough tax revenues to support the reasonable opportunity of every person to reach his or her potential. This standard comes from the book of *Genesis*, revealing that each person is created in God's image with a divinely inspired potential to carry out God's work on earth; these standards can also be found in *Exodus*, *Leviticus*, *Deuteronomy*, *Amos*, *Micah*, and *Isaiah*, mandating the forgiveness of debt, the

---

Susan Pace Hamill is a professor of law at the University of Alabama.

release of servants every seven years, and land tenure rights.[3]

In the ancient Near East, where the first audience received the Old Testament Law, the required seven-year releases and land tenure rights were the reasonable opportunity of their time, guaranteeing that those falling to the bottom, whether it be by bad luck or bad choices, had a reasonable chance to pull themselves up. The reasonable opportunity of our time encompasses a number of areas including adequate education, job training, decent healthcare, and housing.[4] The teachings of Jesus Christ, which fulfill the Law of the Prophets and preach the good news to the poor and release the oppressed, absolutely affirm this moral requirement.[5]

Some Christians argue that tax revenues should only fund the "minimum state" (e.g., roads, police, the courts, national defense), because charity, especially from the churches, will adequately cover other public needs. This argument cannot be theologically defended because it denies the Fall of humankind, which brought evil and sin, including the sin of greed, into the world. Our inescapable tendency to succumb to the sin of greed means that most of us will never voluntarily pay our fair share of the revenues needed to fund the reasonable opportunity of all Americans to develop their divinely inspired potential .[6]

When evaluating how the tax burden should be allocated,

it is useful first to define the options. Regressive taxes proportionally impose greater burdens at smaller income levels, especially among the poor and lower middle classes. Of the variety of flat tax models being discussed, only those that shield income at poverty levels and prevent regressive effects among the lower middle classes are credible. The difference between credible flat taxes and progressive taxes is that credible flat taxes impose the same proportional tax burden among the middle classes and the wealthy, while progressive taxes require the tax burden to increase proportionally as income levels rise.[7]

When morally evaluating tax burdens under the standards of biblical justice, we must start with *Genesis*, which reveals God as the sole creator and ultimate owner of all the earth's wealth and resources, with human beings serving as tenants and stewards for God's purposes. Private property rights, while generally recognized and respected, do not outweigh all other moral concerns.[8]

The Bible also provides more detailed moral principles guiding how tax burdens should be allocated. Tax laws that impose tax burdens on those in poverty—or that allocate the tax burden in a manner that causes regressive effects on the lower middle classes when compared to those enjoying higher income levels—are immoral under the Judeo-Christian principle forbidding oppression. The general Judeo-Christian teachings, especially found in the Gospel of *Luke*, on the greater moral obligations of those blessed with greater amounts of wealth, absolutely condemn flat models as immoral, and they require tax burdens to be allocated under a moderately progressive model. Despite shielding income at poverty levels and preventing regressive effects among the lower middle classes, credible flat models ignore these teachings because the wealthiest taxpayers enjoy the greatest benefits at the significant expense of the middles classes.[9]

Jesus Christ emphasized that following him would involve substantial sacrifice. Dr. Frank Thielman, one of my professors at the Beeson Divinity School, metaphorically describes this as holding on to one's wealth with a "light grip." In a democracy, where the tax laws are a product of our political participation, this requires those of us at higher levels of income and wealth to support tax policy that imposes greater, sometimes substantially greater, tax burdens than competing tax policy structures, which fall short of Judeo-Christian ethical standards.[10]

The greater level of sacrifice that Judeo-Christian–guided tax policy requires of the wealthy and powerful marks tax policy as one of the most important barometers measuring the authenticity of our faith. Those at higher levels of income and wealth who divorce tax policy issues from their faith and confine faith-based wealth issues to voluntary charity, in addition to denying the Fall of humankind, are implicitly assuming that their own efforts, rather than God's grace, provide the ability to produce wealth.[11]

The moral principles of Judeo-Christian ethics cannot be invoked to support tax policy laws seeking to foster equality of result by massively re-distributing wealth. The greater levels of sacrifice required of those at greater levels of income and wealth must be balanced against reasonable rights to enjoy private property, as well as individual autonomy and freedom. The Old Testament Law does not contemplate any degree of utopian equality and implicitly assumes that a significant level of personal responsibility and individual effort will be necessary to take advantage of educational and other opportunities. And the New Testament's teachings are eschatological, meaning the full extent of God's standards of justice will not materialize until Jesus comes again.[12]

The moral principles of Judeo-Christian ethics do not provide precise tax policy answers. Rather they offer guidelines for engaging in discussion, recognizing that reasonable people of faith will disagree on the details ironing out the precise level of revenues and allocation of the tax burden. The moral conversation needs to keep these general principles at the forefront: adequate revenues are required to support reasonable opportunity, and the tax burden must be moderately progressive. We always need to be asking whether the wealthy and powerful are paying their fair share, especially if contemplated changes reduce their share. This is because the sin of greed will drive the wealthy and powerful to go to great lengths to avoid their fair share. If we are not vigilant, their political clout will cause tax policy to drift away from Judeo-Christian values.[13]

President Bush's first-term tax policy, which dished out tax cuts overwhelmingly benefiting the wealthiest Americans while contributing to enormous federal deficits threatening federal funding cuts in areas that uplift poor and middle-class Americans, raises very troubling Judeo-Christian moral issues. The reasons for justifying these tax cuts and the push to make them permanent are even more alarming. In addition to defending the tax cuts using the disreputable theory of supply-side economics, which claims that the tax cuts will cause economic growth, the discussion surrounding tax policy at the highest federal levels exalts private property rights above all other concerns, reflecting the values of objectivist ethics, a form of atheism that worships the individual.[14]

Objectivist ethics deems that each person acting in his or her rational self-interest is the only avenue to reach moral correctness. The principles of objectivist ethics value personal autonomy and assume that the individual alone produces wealth—with no concept of God's grace being the source of our talents to produce wealth, or of God being the ultimate owner of all wealth, or of human beings having any moral obligations to God and to other human beings. The values of objectivist ethics support tax cuts principally benefiting the wealthy and promote flat models and reduced government spending capable of covering only the minimum state.[15]

We have the most vocal, faith-oriented president in recent memory resorting to atheistic values when leading the country's tax policy. This is a gross violation of the moral obligations of his faith, and it is a disgrace. But he is not the only one. Many members of Congress supported the tax cuts, and many Americans did so as well. As of this writing, I am engaged in a massive research project on the state and local tax policy trends of the fifty states, and preliminarily it appears that the tax laws in most states conclusively violate the moral principles of Judeo-Christian ethics.[16]

Why is our tax policy continuing to move further away from reflecting genuine Judeo-Christian values? Religion, Christianity especially, has become a low-sacrifice operation. Too many religious leaders have limited faith-based ethics to issues of personal piety and low-sacrifice public policy issues. These are cultural issues that, while raising significant theological concerns where reasonable people of faith can and do disagree, ultimately involve little or no personal sacrifice. Gay marriage is a good example of a low-sacrifice issue.[17]

Limiting the pro-life agenda to the issue of whether abortion should be legal or illegal is the most hypocritical example of a low-sacrifice issue masquerading as faith-based justice. Regardless of your view of the legal issue, you cannot claim to be truly pro-life unless you are also willing to fight for the high sacrifice of Judeo-Christian–guided tax policy. Adequate tax revenues are essential to embracing the dignity of life, which includes funding prenatal care and nutrition for all mothers, fighting poverty, and providing adequate education opportunities for all children.[18]

The teachings of Jesus and the Hebrew prophets make it quite clear that a community using low-sacrifice issues to cover up injustice will disintegrate by the weight of its own greed. Alabama is an example of this. We have one of the nation's most immoral state and local tax structures and have suffered devastating consequences in the form of well below average K–12 funding and performance indicators, declining job prospectives for those with less education and skill and high rates of poverty, infant mortality, and many other health problems.[19]

In 2003 Alabama's Republican governor, Bob Riley, proposed a major tax reform plan that failed at the polls by a 2:1 margin.[20] Perhaps racked with anger and emotion, and without the ability to distinguish the lies and distortions of the opposition from the truth, the very people who would have been helped the most by this plan voted against it. Alabama's immoral tax policy has rendered many of our people unable to improve their own situation using the tools of democracy.[21]

All people of faith, especially religious leaders, must rise up and demand that the atheistic values of objectivist ethics poisoning our tax-policy discussions and decisions be purged and replaced with genuine Judeo-Christian values. Only spiritual renewal has a chance to combat the powerful forces of greed currently leading us astray. If the church fails to embrace tax policy as one of the most important public policy issues of faith, the whole country will face the downward spiral that we are already witnessing in Alabama, despite the efforts of numerous good Alabamians, as well as my own, to remedy the terrible injustice poisoning our state. Adam Cohen of the *New York Times* put it more plainly: "As goes Alabama, so may go the nation."[22]

3

They can strengthen the economy
Economists Find That the Right Taxes Support Growth

Jeff Madrick

One of the more damaging pieces of conventional wisdom that has arisen over the past quarter century in America is that big government and high taxes undermine our national prosperity. Bigger government, the argument goes, reduces the rate of economic growth when it borrows money to pay for itself because this crowds out private investment. And if government raises taxes instead, that reduces incentives to invest and work. Slower growth means lower wages, weak profits, and fewer jobs overall. Even progressives sometimes cast government as an impediment to growth; they argue that while funding social programs may cost us jobs and higher incomes, this is an economic price worth paying for a just and decent society.

Readers may be surprised to find out that there is no unambiguous evidence to support the view that high taxes inhibit growth. As New York University professor and

---

Jeff Madrick is the editor of *Challenge Magazine*.

former World Bank economist William Easterly wrote, "You can make a theoretical case that high taxes impede economic growth, but it is just not supported by the evidence in the U.S. or across countries."[1] Easterly is a mainstream economist, best described as a centrist.

People who make claims about the costs of big government do so with such confidence that you'd think proving their case would be awfully easy. If they are right, higher taxes should take a serious, easily measurable chunk out of the economy. But they cannot find evidence to support their claims. The best empirical studies do not show a large loss, nor do they show that high taxes are associated with slower growth or low taxes with higher growth. To the contrary, some recent research support the notion that taxes, fairly collected and well spent, actually *promote* economic growth and, importantly in today's economy, support the creation of jobs that pay decent wages.[2]

Despite the conventional wisdom, we can and often have had a decent society, big government, and prosperity side by side. How can this be? The answer may be that government invests taxes in areas that are essential to economic growth, such as education, transportation infrastructure, healthcare, and basic science. A strong government can also create confidence in a society and assure a reasonable distribution of the benefits of growth.

The politicians who shape our economic policies, and the economists they call upon to support their cases, have accustomed us to thinking of tax *cuts* as the answer to our economic problems. But a cursory look at American history tells us this is untrue. The best modern example is in the post–World War II period. The United States taxed its well-to-do citizens at much higher rates in the 1950s and 1960s than today. Average tax rates for the top 5 percent of earners was over 34 percent and the marginal tax rate for those making over $400,000 hovered at approximately 91 percent.[3] Yet the nation enjoyed the fastest real average gains to economic growth in its history during these two decades, with decadal growth rates of 0.96 and 1.18 percent respectively.[4]

U.S. economic history is full of such examples of tax-payer-funded government interventions that have promoted growth. Alexander Hamilton, the founding father of business, sought to protect domestic manufacturing from foreign competition through taxes on imports. He also wanted a powerful federal government, that could sell its own bonds to build the roads the nation badly needed and could invest revenues from tariffs and land sales into domestic businesses. Even followers of Thomas Jefferson, who originally opposed government support for industrial expansion, eventually became interventionists. The Jeffersonian Republicans in New York, for example, used government money to build one of the greatest public projects of the time, the Erie Canal, which was completed in 1825.

During the course of the nineteenth century, when the

U.S. federal and state bureaucracies were still tiny, governments used tax dollars to build the canals, subsidize the railroads, and develop a widely envied public education system. By 1850, America's free primary schools were better attended than those of any other nation.

The United States' historical investment in education is of particular relevance to current economic debates. It has been argued, with good reason, that universal education supports a vibrant democracy by promoting citizen capacity to understand, communicate about, and cast well-informed votes on public issues. But a publicly funded school system can also be seen as a key ingredient in the country's economic success, one that helped new immigrants turn the grueling Industrial Revolution into a springboard for the formation of a large and growing middle class.

Recent work in development economics continues to identify investment in education as a crucial factor separating countries that grow from those that don't. According to Edward L. Glaeser of Harvard University and Albert Saiz of the University of Pennsylvania, "Aside from climate, skill composition may be the most powerful predictor of growth."[5]

Inadequate and unequally distributed investment in U.S. public schools is especially frustrating given that, unlike most other policy solutions to economic problems, education actually seems to work. Although the situation is complex, the data on the benefits of higher education are convincing. According to the 2000 census, for example, the median income of an American man with a college degree was about $52,200, 60 percent higher than the $31,600 for those with only a high school degree. The proportions are about the same for women. The average incomes of workers with only high school degrees have fallen substantially since the 1970s.

Evidence suggests that even bigger social returns can be earned by investing in earlier education—ideally, before kindergarten. A wide range of researchers believe that public investment in good pre-K programs pay for themselves many times over; reports of the returns from current programs, such as federally funded Head Start, are already demonstrating their cost-effectiveness.

Good evidence also exists that efficient investment in public transportation infrastructure pays handsome social dividends. Ishaq Nadiri, an economist at New York University, and Theofanis P. Mamuneas of the University of Cyprus show that the rates of return on such public investments are equal to or even better than the rates of return on private capital.[6]

What economists call natural experiments reinforce claims that high taxes do not impede growth. An economist from the famously pro-market University of Chicago, Nancy L. Stokey, along with Sergio Rebelo of Northwestern University, made use of historical changes in the income tax to study its impact on the economy. Income tax revenue in the

United States rose from about 2 percent of Gross Domestic Product (GDP) in 1913, when the income tax was first introduced by constitutional amendment, to 15 percent of GDP in 1942. What happened to growth as a result of this new and relatively fast-growing tax burden? In the words of Stokey and Rebelo: "This large rise in income tax rates produced no noticeable effect on the average growth rate of the economy."[7]

U.S. economic history since World War II provides another natural experiment about the impact of taxes on growth. Total taxes as a proportion of GDP stayed relatively flat during the postwar boom and through the marked economic slowdown of the early 1970s. But the composition of taxes then changed. Marginal rates fell for the rich much more than they did for the middle class and poor over this period. In the early 1980s, in particular, tax cuts by President Ronald Reagan plus increases in payroll taxes made the U.S. system considerably less progressive than it was in the 1950s and 1960s. If lower taxes for the rich do indeed raise incentives to entrepreneurialism, as anti-tax proponents argue, the economy should have grown faster during the Reagan period. Instead, it grew more slowly.

The experience of other nations adds considerable weight to the argument that the level of taxes has little long-term effect on growth. Joel Slemrod of the University of Michigan and his co-author, Jon Bakija, compared GDP per capita with the level of taxes in the two dozen or so member nations of the Organization for Economic Cooperation and Development (OECD) in their 2004 book, *Taxing Ourselves*.[8] They find that growth occurred both in relatively low-tax nations such as the United States and Japan and in high-tax nations such as Scandinavia. Their findings contradict earlier studies that purported to show that high taxes reduced growth rates. "Looking at taxes only is only one-half of the story," Mr. Slemrod said. "If government raised taxes but then spent the money poorly, the economy would grow more slowly."[9] On the other hand, high-tax countries may spend tax revenue effectively and promote growth in the process.

The startling lack of evidence that taxes impede economic growth does not necessarily mean high taxes are good for the economy. But economic historian Peter H. Lindert of the University of California at Davis finds that under certain circumstances, taxes have been beneficial for growth. In his book, *Growing Public*, Lindert extends Slemrod's analysis, examining levels of public investment in education, transportation, and healthcare, and such transfers as Social Security, and finds a stark contradiction between conventional wisdom and the evidence.[10] He writes, "It is well known that higher taxes and transfers reduce productivity. Well known—but unsupported by statistics and history."[11]

Lindert compares the level of social spending (as opposed to the level of overall government spending) over nine decades, from 1910 to 2000, in nineteen developed nations, including most of western Europe, Japan, Australia, the United States, and Canada. In addition to finding that high spending on social programs did not slow productivity growth or per capita GDP, he observes that many high-tax European welfare states grew *faster* than the United States, a nation with low social spending. This finding flies in the face of the theory that tax-funded social programs deter investments and blunt willingness to work.[12]

Some economists, including Lindert, reason that the tax systems of countries with high social spending may be pro-growth partially as a result of deriving substantial revenues from sales taxes, thus suppressing consumption and raising national savings. At the same time nations in Scandinavia and continental Europe do not tax profits and capital investment any more than the United States or Japan does, and in some cases even less so. Nations with high social spending typically attach high taxes to such "bad" products as alcohol, tobacco, and gasoline, Lindert notes, which contributes to better health and environmental quality and therefore greater productivity and less costly environmental regulations.

Another important difference between the United States and higher-tax countries may be political: social programs in nations with high welfare levels usually include everyone. Because benefits are generally not cut off as incomes grow, funding for social programs enjoys broader public support.

Finally, much of the public spending in these nations—on education, healthcare, family leave, and childcare—is directly conducive to economic growth. For example, comprehensive public health programs help people live more economically productive lives.[13]

The idea that spending tax revenue on the right things can actually promote growth gets an additional boost from Harvard University's James Medoff, who studies the job-creating benefits of different categories of public spending.[14] Medoff created a measure that estimates the number of jobs produced by a dollar of spending and the level of pay and benefits those jobs provide, combining the two results into a labor market "score." He examined how capital investment, consumption, and various government-spending programs scored, that is, added good jobs to the economy.

Private investment in durable goods did especially well, creating jobs that pay above average wages. But the nation's spending on education programs did even better, creating many more jobs per dollar spent. And the jobs paid fairly well, if not as well as jobs derived from capital spending. Government healthcare spending also produced many well-paying jobs. Other government spending programs associated with good job growth funded highways, water and air facilities, and police and firefighters. Military spending also added good jobs but not at an equivalent rate. The lowest-score spending on average was consumption, exactly the type of expenditure that is driving the economy today.

The good news from all these studies is that we can indeed use tax policy to promote economic growth, and we can do so without tax cuts that balloon the deficit. Extra government spending that is channeled into the areas that contribute to economic growth can decrease the federal deficit by funding social policies that promote more growth than they deter. The bad news is that since 2000, we have followed exactly the opposite course by implementing enormous tax cuts, which were unable to produce a net gain in jobs or to raise wages at a normal pace. In other words, we chose to pursue a more costly, less effective growth strategy even though better options were available.

In the meantime much work has been left undone. Changes over the last thirty years make the next administration's position on the role of taxes in the economy a high-stakes issue. The two-worker family has become the norm. Technology and globalization have made job loss in certain sectors inevitable. Corporate success and higher productivity no longer translate into higher wages. One of today's quintessentially successful companies, Wal-Mart, has made the ruthless reduction of labor costs a central part of its strategy. Unlike General Motors, which (thanks to good management, rapid growth, and a heavily unionized labor force) produced high-paying jobs in its prime, what's good for Wal-Mart is likely to be bad for large sections of the U.S. labor force.

In addition to the poor and working class not faring well, many of those in the middle are having trouble making ends meet. For many families, even when both spouses work, the costs of education, healthcare, and housing continue to rise much faster than median family incomes.

If politicians are open to the best that economics has to teach, they will understand that raising taxes moderately to pay for social programs would improve quality of life for a broad swath of the American public *and also* help the economy grow. The question is whether politicians will have the sense and courage to break with the powerful anti-tax lobby and their favorite ideological economists and put some of these ideas into practice. A just society can be a prosperous society. In the long run an unjust society that does not invest in the human potential of its people, probably cannot be.

4

Excellent public schools depend on taxes
Money, Schools, and Justice

Stan Karp

For the past thirty years, battles over school funding have been clogging the nation's courts. Ever since the U.S. Supreme Court declared in 1973 (*San Antonio v. Rodriguez*) that education was not a fundamental right protected by the U.S. Constitution, equity advocates have fought a state-by-state battle against the "savage inequalities" of school finance systems that provide sharply different levels of education to students from different class, race, and community backgrounds.[1]

Typically, inequities have been traced to wide gaps in per-pupil spending and to finance systems that rely heavily on local property taxes. More recently, "adequacy" cases have focused on the gap between what school funding systems provide and what state and federal education standards (including the No Child Left Behind [NCLB] law) demand of schools.[2] School funding systems both mirror and reproduce the inequality we see all around us.

Stan Karp is an editor of *Rethinking Schools*.

The details are complicated. But the heart of the matter is simple: our schools don't get enough money, and the money they do get is not distributed fairly. Beneath the legal jargon and complex legislative formulas that dominate debate over school finance lie two central questions: (1) Will we provide schools with the resources they need to make high-quality education possible? and (2) Will we provide those resources to all children, or only some children? The answers we give will go a long way toward determining whether our society's future will be one of democratic promise or deepening division.

Since the early 1970s, more than forty state high courts have issued decisions in school finance cases. About half have declared existing funding systems illegal or inadequate and mandated a variety of corrective measures.[3]

But as New Jersey's Education Law Center has pointed out, "Law books are filled with wonderful paper victories which have never been implemented."[4] While glaring disparities in school funding may persuade judges to order reform, it's been difficult to prevent governors and state legislators from limiting the impact of court orders. Restrained by separation-of-powers concerns and a conservative political climate, most courts have given states wide latitude to proceed with half measures and evasive action.

In some states tentative steps toward equity taken under court pressure have been thwarted by the rising tide of anti-tax populism. California is a prime example. The state's 1972 *Serrano* decision was one of the first rulings that required a state to correct massive inequities among districts in educational services.[5] Some efforts were made to equalize spending by revising aid formulas and transferring some property tax revenues from wealthier to poorer districts. But these efforts were derailed by Proposition 13, a 1978 ballot initiative, which capped property taxes in one of the opening rounds of the "tax revolt" that came to shape local, state, and federal tax policy in the 1980s and 1990s (and which, despite promises of relief to hard-pressed taxpayers, has succeeded primarily in swelling government budget deficits, starving public services, and redirecting wealth upward). As a result of Proposition 13, the state of California was forced to assume a greater share of local school spending, which did lead to a degree of greater "equity" among districts. But there was also a dramatic decline in spending on schools in California relative to other states. In the 1960s, California was fifth in per-pupil spending; by the end of the 1990s it was thirtieth, well below the national average. Class size in California grew to among the highest in the nation. Because of Proposition 13 and its offspring, support for California schools tended toward "equalization" at a level that kept them in a state of perpetual budgetary crisis.[6]

The property tax issue is both a root problem and a distraction from the core issues of adequacy and equity. Local property taxes still supply about 43 percent of all school funds. State support varies, but on average provides about 49 percent. The federal government's share of education spending, despite the huge impact of federal policies like NCLB, is still only about 8 percent.[7]

The unequal distribution of property in the United States and the high levels of race and class segregation make it inevitable that schools heavily dependent on local property taxes will be unequal. With more than 16,000 separate school districts, the reliance on property taxes functions as a sorting mechanism for class and race privilege, allowing pockets of "elite schooling" to exist within the public system.

Any real chance of increasing and redistributing education resources requires fundamentally changing the connection between school spending and local property taxes. This reliance on local property taxes creates strong budgetary pressure for austerity. When school budgets are presented like sacrificial lambs to hard-pressed local taxpayers (who never get to vote on tax abatements for developers or whether the U.S. Defense Department should build another aircraft carrier), the budget process often is driven not by what schools and students need, but by a desire to keep the tax rate flat. When only a fraction of the local population has children in the schools, and an even smaller fraction (about 15 percent) usually votes in budget referendums, the politics of school financing works to undercut quality education and to keep communities divided.

Still, growing efforts to find alternatives are sparked by court orders, heavy local tax burdens, and the ongoing national debate about education reform. One set of fiscal reform proposals is geared to redistributing property tax revenues from richer districts to poorer ones. Another set of proposals seeks to replace property taxes with other taxes—often sales taxes—and to have the state assume a larger fraction of overall school spending. Still other proposals involve redefining state aid formulas, so they are calculated in ways that promote greater equalization.

The problem is that no particular financial mechanism, in itself, guarantees either equity or quality in education. Relying on progressive income and corporate taxes, instead of regressive property and sales taxes, is a fairer way to raise revenues. But using a fairer revenue source does not mean that adequate funds will be made available. A number of states adopted new formulas promising better funding only to see them cut once the higher costs became clear. If the underlying motivation is a desire to cut taxes or to hold down educational spending, rather than to promote quality and equity, it may not matter which fiscal mechanism is chosen to do the job.

Another response has been to try to define what an "adequate" education means, and then to peg funding formulas to the cost of providing it. Here again, debate persists over what level of educational services the state is obligated to provide for all.

This tension is reflected in New Jersey's *Abbott* decisions, which are arguably the most progressive rulings for poor urban schools in the history of school finance cases.[8] Initially, the case covered familiar territory. The New Jersey Supreme Court ruled that the state's system of school funding, which relies heavily on unequal property tax bases in nearly 600 separate districts, denied children in urban areas equal access to the "thorough and efficient" education guaranteed by the New Jersey constitution. The Education Law Center documented gross inequality and pressing need in urban districts, and the court established unequivocally that it was the state's obligation to redress this inequality.

Where *Abbott* really blazed new ground was in the standard it set for this equity mandate. Throughout long years of litigation, the court repeatedly pressed the state to define the essential elements of a "thorough and efficient" education. Repeatedly, successive state administrations avoided this request, fearing that a generous definition would obligate them to provide such resources to poor districts, while a low estimate would require explaining why the state's most successful districts were spending much more.

The state tried changing the subject from "money" to "standards." It adopted "core curriculum content standards" and argued that if all districts implemented these standards, all students would receive an equally adequate education. Essentially, the court responded: nice try, but no sale. Standards may be helpful in defining educational expectations and outcomes, it reasoned, but they are not a substitute for the programs, staff, and resources needed to reach them. When the court looked closely at the funding formula passed by the state legislature to support the new standards, the numbers looked suspiciously like political calculations designed to keep state school aid at or near existing levels without redressing the record of inequality the court had before it.

Frustrated by the state's evasions, the New Jersey court ultimately devised its own formula. The court took as its equity standard the level of spending in the state's richest and most successful school districts. Arguing that these districts obviously knew what was needed for kids to succeed, the court ordered the state to raise per-pupil spending in the poorest urban districts to the average level of the 130 richest. And citing deeper social problems and the cumulative effects of concentrated poverty, the court ordered "supplemental funding" in poor districts for programs like full-day pre-K, summer school, and tutoring, above and beyond parity for regular educational programs. *Abbott* remains "the first decision in the history of school finance reform to establish an equality standard for the allocation of education resources to poor urban children."[9] Moreover, the court's decision was phrased in striking language that made clear the larger implications it was addressing: "The fact is that a large part of our society is disintegrating, so large a part that it cannot help but affect the rest. Everyone's future is at stake, and not just the poor's."[10]

This extraordinary decision opened up a new era of reform in New Jersey's urban districts. While battles over implementation and budgetary issues continue, significant progress has been made since *Abbott* funding started to flow in the late 1990s. More than 40,000 three- and four-year-olds now attend high-quality, full-day pre-K and kindergarten programs. The math and language test score gap between urban and suburban fourth graders has been cut in half. New Jersey boasts the highest high school graduation rates in the country, including the highest rates for African American and Hispanic students (though significant gaps among groups and communities remain).[11]

But while *Abbott* brought long overdue equity to the thirty-one poor urban districts that were parties to the case, it did not fix the state's overall school finance system. More than 400 "middle districts" remain squeezed by property tax formulas and perpetual state budget crisis. Poor rural districts and "Abbott rim" districts, which border designated Abbott districts and have substantial populations of poor and special needs students, have had little success gaining access to *Abbott* levels of funding.

In fact, New Jersey's experience underscores the contradiction between equity goals and school funding systems based on local property taxes. The state is among the highest spenders on education and has the best funding levels for poor schools. But it ranks forty-first out of fifty states in the total share of local school costs picked up at the state level: about 40 percent.[12] Because *Abbott* directed a larger portion of this state aid to the poorest districts, suburban and rural districts were pitted against one another in competition for an increasingly inadequate pool of state funds. State aid to non–*Abbott* districts has remained flat for five years, making them more dependent than ever on raising local property taxes, which are now the highest in the nation.[13] Unless New Jersey adopts a new school funding formula that significantly increases state share and reduces reliance on local property taxes, sustaining both the *Abbott* commitments and New Jersey's status as a leader in educational achievement will be increasingly difficult.

Almost monthly a prominent academic or government agency issues a report emphasizing the importance of public education to some aspect of our nation's future, from global competitiveness to national security to multicultural harmony. But the main prerequisite for improving this critical social institution is a funding system that provides high-quality schooling for all kids through sustainable and fair tax policies. In the long run this means moving away from systems that rely on local property taxes toward regional, state, and federal funding sources.

Realistically, to make good on promises of educational equity and excellence will require tens of billions of dollars over many years, the amount of funds, for example, that have been poured into the military for decades. In 2005–06, total K–12 education spending in the United States was about $500 billion. The latest proposed military budget for FY 2008 is $622 billion. Public and private reports have documented a need for more than $300 billion in construction and renovation of K–12 facilities. (Costs that are generally not included in the per-pupil expenditures that are the focus of most equalization efforts.) And putting aside for the moment the many dubious aspects of the NCLB law, studies indicate that even to approach NCLB's inappropriate and fanciful goal of 100 percent proficiency for all students on state tests by 2014 would require an annual increase in school spending of about $130 billion above current levels, about ten times the current size of Title I, the largest federal education program.[14]

Only a national effort to reform social investment and tax policies can generate such resources. That means public campaigns to put new state and federal tax policies behind the nation's lofty educational rhetoric. It also means broader public efforts to reorder the nation's social priorities. That, after all, is what excellence and equity in school funding is ultimately all about.

5

Taxes help families raise kids
Using Tax Policy to Support Family Work

Nancy Folbre

You'd think that proponents of family values would appreciate the value of family work. Raising kids, taking care of sick family members or friends, helping the elderly get by— these are all productive activities. When we can't do them ourselves, we usually have to pay someone to do them in our place.

But many people don't like to admit that unpaid work is work, because then they can no longer claim that "welfare mothers" are simply too lazy to have a paid job; they can no longer argue that a progressive income tax discourages work (what it does is reduce the benefits of paid work relative to untaxed family work); and they can no longer bluster that paid family leave from work would reduce economic growth.

Most people appreciate the contribution that unpaid care makes to our economic system. In business terms, invest-

Nancy Folbre is a professor of economics at the University of Massachusetts, Amherst, and a staff economist with the Center for Popular Economics.

ments in the production and maintenance of human capital improve our living standards. Unfortunately, businesses tend to take the investments that families and friends make in one another for granted—assuming that people (primarily women) will continue to make them no matter what.

But the costs of raising and educating children are going up. Older people, living longer, require more assistance than they once did. Most adults doing paid work also do care work, juggling the two but often forced to put their paycheck first.

A number of specific government policies, such as paid family leave from work and high-quality universal childcare, could help address these problems. We could redesign our income and Social Security tax system to provide consistent support for care outside the market economy.

Skeptics sometimes argue that Americans will never agree to the kinds of government spending common in Sweden and other northern European countries. But to some extent, we already have. We just don't spend our money very effectively. Carefully designed reforms could make our tax dollars go farther.

Principles of the Family Welfare State

The libertarian rhetoric that describes taxes as a form of theft is based on a form of individualism that denies our obligation to others. But no society can reproduce itself without enforcing its obligations to dependents. The economic rationale for the family welfare state grows out of the material benefits that flow from social insurance and investment in human capabilities.

Nations, like families, inherit assets from the past and invest for the future. Much of our social spending represents an intergenerational transfer. Working-age adults pay taxes that metaphorically "pay back" public money spent on them as children and "pay forward" the resources that will be devoted to them when they are elderly.

Individuals can also save, borrow, and invest, but we all benefit by pooling some of our resources. Insurance systems work best when risks are widely spread. No one knows when they might lose a parent, be abandoned by a spouse, give birth to a disabled child, or find themselves in need of long-term care.

Our economic futures depend upon investments in our own human capabilities and those of the people we live and work with. The time and money parents devote to children literally produce human capital. Families provide important healthcare services. The elderly do not cease contributing to our society when they retire from paid employment. Their accomplishments inspire us, and their wisdom informs us.

An effective and sustainable social-insurance system works, like a healthy family, on principles of solidarity and reciprocity. Everybody contributes, and everybody benefits. The problem with our current system is that many important contributions go unrecognized, and many benefits are unfairly distributed. Changes in tax policy can address these imbalances, promoting a healthier and more productive relationship between the paid and unpaid work that supports individual, family, and social life.

Paid Family Leave from Work

Thanks to landmark legislation passed under the Clinton administration, many American workers (those who work for a firm with more than fifty employees) have a right to twelve weeks unpaid leave from work to cope with their own illness or to help care for a child. But relatively few parents can afford to take time off. Most countries provide *paid* family leaves from work, and America should, too.

Some states, such as California, have taken the lead, using the funds from their disability insurance system to provide partial wage replacement for individuals who need time off to tend to family. A federal family-leave insurance program could be combined with improvements to existing disability and unemployment insurance systems—currently a confusing mess of programs that impose high bureaucratic costs on businesses without providing adequate coverage for most workers.

Childcare

Working parents rely heavily on childcare both for preschool age children and for summers and after-school.

Even families with a parent who stays home rely on child-care to help educate and socialize their kids. But high-quality childcare is hard to find and even harder to pay for. Full-time care often costs more than tuition and fees at a state university. Subsidized care is limited to low-income families, and waiting lists are long.

Practical models for improvement abound. Many soldiers are parents, and the U.S. armed forces run one of the best childcare systems in the country. Georgia uses a special state lottery to fund virtually universal education for its four year olds. North Carolina's Smart Start program both expands access for children and improves wages and working conditions for childcare workers.

Childcare and early childhood education should be integrated into our larger public school system in ways that encourage the existing diversity of providers but set and support high quality standards.

Education

The goal of the No Child Left Behind Act—to eliminate shocking disparities among children based on race, ethnicity, and class—remains unmet. Schools in low-income neighborhoods often lack the resources they need to improve educational quality. The reliance of public schools on local property taxes—discussed in more detail elsewhere in this volume—bears heavily on the elderly, who tend to own their own homes but live on fixed incomes.

A sounder basis for education financing could come from taxing wealth more broadly, as many European countries do. Real estate now represents a much smaller portion of all wealth than it once did. We could, in addition, tax financial assets—stocks and bonds held primarily by the richest families—and use the proceeds to promote equality of educational opportunity.

Supporting equal educational opportunity also means giving public universities more support. Tuition and fees have risen faster than the rate of inflation, while student aid has tilted away from those most in need. Many young people know they need a college degree to get a decent job in a rapidly globalizing economy, but not all can afford to obtain one. Graduates are typically saddled with burdensome loans, sometimes financed by private companies who have bribed universities to recommend their services. Like our elementary and secondary school system, higher education should be financed collectively.

Income Tax Reform

Both federal and state income taxes offer some support for childrearing in the form of deductions and credits that add up to a significant amount—more than the annual Swedish family allowance of about $1,500 a year per child. But these tax breaks are complicated, inconsistent, and poorly targeted. Poor families benefit most from the Earned Income Tax Credit, but only for their first two children. No extra benefits are provided for third and later children. The rules are much more generous to middle-class and affluent families, many of whom can claim valuable deductions and credits for all their children, as well as a dependent deduction for a luxury that few other families can afford, a stay-at-home spouse. The tax benefits that parents with income of $125,000 a year can claim often add up to more than the tax benefits for parents with a combined income of $40,000.

Many countries, including Canada, the United Kingdom, and Australia, provide tax-based family benefits that are linked to income. But they generally provide more support for families at the bottom of the distribution than America does, and less for families at the top. Conservatives in this country argue that higher tax rates on high-earning individuals would create disincentives for them to put in extra hours at the office. But many of these high-fliers could benefit themselves and the rest of us by spending more time working in their families and communities.

In addition to making income taxes more progressive, we could make them simpler and more family-friendly by improving the current system of deductions and credits. The costs of paying for childcare represent a work-related expense for many parents, but they are only allowed to deduct a fraction of these from their taxable income. Deductions for college expenses are both complicated and limited. A comprehensive "Income Tax Reform for Parents

Package" both could increase support for childrearing and simplify the process of filing.

One possibility proposed by Karen Kornbluh, currently policy director for Senator Barack Obama, would extend the tax-free medical and dependent care accounts that some firms currently set up for their employees. Parent accounts would allow parents to set aside the money they spend on childcare, healthcare, and education for their dependents in a special tax-free account. The government could then match a certain percentage of the funds spent, on a sliding scale with greater amounts to low-income families.

Social Security Reform

As noted elsewhere in this volume, most Americans pay more in Social Security taxes than in income taxes. In return, we receive important benefits—survivor's insurance to help care for family members when a wage-earner dies, disability insurance, and inflation-protected security in old age.

But the level of these benefits is determined primarily by the length of time and average earnings in paid employment. The work of raising children—creating the next generation of taxpayers who will pay into the Social Security system—is not officially recognized. Marriage, however, is generously rewarded. An individual who remains married to a high-earner for at least ten years becomes eligible for retirement benefits equivalent to 50 percent of those of the surviving spouse and 100 percent if that spouse has died.

These benefits are provided regardless of whether the recipient has contributed to the Social Security system through paid employment or by raising children.

Single mothers raise more than one-third of the children in this country. Whether unmarried or divorced, they are often forced to take part-time jobs, or take time out of paid employment to care for children. As a result of their reduced earnings record, many are eligible only for very low Social Security payments. They are destined for poverty in old age. Meanwhile, the fathers of their children (who not infrequently escape responsibility for paying child support) have often developed a stronger earnings record. They can expect higher Social Security payments, partly financed by the taxes of children to whose upbringing they contributed relatively little.

A complete solution to this problem would require an improved child-support system and more equitable sharing of parental responsibilities among single parents. But individuals who take time out of paid employment to care for family members could be given caregiver credits that count toward their future pension benefits. Such policies have been implemented in Norway and several other northern European countries. In Germany, for example, childless individuals are required to pay higher pension contributions than others.

Another option might be to use the Social Security system, rather than the state disability/unemployment insurance or the income tax systems, to support family work, allowing individuals essentially to take a "temporary re-tirement" benefit when they need time to care for children or other family members.

Care Insurance for the Elderly

Investments don't stop with the young. We also have a stake in the health and well-being of the older generation, because we will all, at best, become a part of it. Social Se-curity has significantly reduced poverty among the elderly, and Medicare helps meet most of their health needs. But neither of these programs covers the cost of long-term care, whether through provision of home care or support for nursing home expenses.

Most of us will live longer than our parents did, but we will also become more vulnerable to infirmities that require long-term care, such as Alzheimer's disease. Elderly women, who often outlive their friends and spouses, are particularly vulnerable. The Medicaid program provides assistance only to the indigent, often forcing individuals to "spend down" their assets by selling their homes. Private long-term care insurance is both expensive and risky. An efficient system of publicly provided long-term care insurance could be designed to encourage in-home and community-based care.

Ending Poverty Among Children

Income inequality is greater in the United States than in most other affluent countries, and child poverty is also higher. Our "policy efforts" in this respect have been weak compared with those of most other affluent countries. The so-called welfare reforms of 1996 were designed primarily to push single mothers off public assistance, not to help them or their children.

A wealth of social-science research shows that poverty hurts kids, reducing their chances of succeeding in school and in later life. Poverty in the United States traps families in a vicious cycle that reproduces racial/ethnic disparities and makes a mockery of equal opportunity. While providing greater support for all parents and improving educational access would reduce the problem of child poverty, these actions would not solve it.

The British Labour Party has launched a major initiative to eliminate child poverty by 2020. A combination of income transfers, tax breaks, childcare, and work incentives set into place to achieve this result has already achieved considerable success. We should launch a similar initiative in the United States. As UK Labour Party leader Gordon Brown emphasizes, children comprise a small part of our population, but a large part of our future.

6

Pollution taxes may save life on earth
Energy Independence and Controlled Global Warming Through Tax Reform

John M. Fitzgerald and Daphne Wysham

Dependence on fossil fuels gives the United States major environmental and security problems. Not only do we mass-produce harmful greenhouse gases and other pollutants, but we also spend heavily on military defense of fuel supplies. These problems will only grow more serious as human-induced climate change contributes to increasingly volatile weather patterns including droughts and floods, worsening conflict over scarce resources, and generating social and economic instability.

Well-designed tax reform can help address these problems without increasing overall tax bills by speeding our

The views in this article are those of Ms. Wysham and Mr. Fitzgerald and do not necessarily reflect the position of the Society for Conservation Biology, where Mr. Fitzgerald has become policy director since this article was written. Daphne Wysham is a fellow and board member of the Institute for Policy Studies.

transition from an economy that fuels pollution, climate change, and conflict to one that supports new jobs, a healthy environment, and energy independence. We already have the technical knowledge needed to put the right tax reforms in place. This chapter lays out the key elements of those reforms.

Reaching our goal of "Climate and Energy Security" means dramatically reducing the use of fossil fuels through a rapid phase-down in carbon-intensive energy consumption and phase-in of clean, renewable energy. And it means simultaneously helping other countries do the same through climate-friendly tariffs and trade and transparent aid and lending.

Shift Taxes to Promote Efficiency

Most experts acknowledge that the United States can achieve major increases in efficiency with existing technology, given the right economic signals and market information. A tax shift—phasing in taxes on carbon and other pollutants and certain resource uses while simultaneously lowering other taxes—would provide incentives for energy efficiency in a revenue-neutral manner. Tools for making green investments less costly, such as tax credits or other tax advantages for energy-efficient capital improvements, would speed the transition along even faster. Taxes can complement legal limits or caps by applying both pressure and rewards for cutting pollution below permitted levels.

In general, tax-based strategies could serve as a guardrail, steering us toward a sustainable, secure path for meeting our energy needs.

Get "Dirty" Fuel Off the Dole

Until now, taxes have in many ways functioned as a barrier keeping us off that path. Massive, hidden subsidies have been an important secret ingredient in the commercial success of fossil fuels. The Congressional Research Service, for example, found $4.25 billion in direct tax subsidies for conventional fossil fuels projected for fiscal year 2005 alone.[1] From the late 1940s to the late 1990s, nuclear and fossil fuels together received between $115 and $147 billion in subsidies compared to renewables' $5 billion.[2] President Bush signed legislation in 2006 that reduced the royalties that oil companies pay for offshore oil production and virtually eliminated royalties on oil from shale.[3]

And those are only some of the *direct* subsidies. Indirect subsidies for oil and gas are huge but harder to measure. According to testimony from the National Defense Council Foundation (NDCF) presented before the Senate Foreign Relations Committee in 2006, Americans pay a hidden price for oil of more than twice the gas pump price, largely due to the public expense of defending our access to oil abroad and over the sea-lanes.[4] The NDCF estimated expenditures for imports of crude oil at $320 billion for 2006 and put the overall cost, including the costs of the military protecting our access and supply lines, at more than twice that figure. This is equivalent to roughly $1,000 per person per year in the United States.

Shifting subsidies from fossil fuels to renewables would reduce these hidden costs and the conflicts associated with them. If, in addition to removing subsidies, we tax fossil fuels to reflect and reduce their social and environmental costs, we can generate revenue, save billions of dollars in avoided future costs, protect valuable ecosystems and generate new jobs in the growing market for clean energy products and services.[5]

Make Renewables the Source for New Energy

In addition to discouraging "dirty" technology, taxes can play a key role in promoting clean energy sources. The U.S. Department of Energy (DOE) reported as early as 1991 that wind farms in just three or four states could produce as much electric energy as the United States used at that time.[6] Since that study was conducted, improvements in wind turbine design have more than doubled the average production capacity of the largest commercial turbines.[7] Meeting our current level of electric energy needs through renewables such as wind and solar power would eliminate more than one-third of the climate-changing and health-damaging air pollution that U.S. sources emit. Emissions would fall even more if we were to use renewables-based electricity for most of our transportation and other energy needs.

Tax policy, in the form of credits and subsidies, played a critical role in bringing wind technology to market. Production tax credits of 1.5 cents[8] per kilowatt-hour helped to promote the development of wind farms across the country and to establish wind as a mainstream option for new power generation—the second largest source of new power in the country for 2005 and 2006, according to the Energy Information Administration.

Although subsidies remain important, technological improvements and growing demand are making renewable technology more cost-competitive. Wind power costs as little as 3 cents, and on average 6–7 cents, per kilowatt-hour— one-third less than the price of electricity generated from new coal plants and competitive with the price of power from older coal plants or natural gas plants.[9] Wind, unlike oil, gas, and uranium, is virtually unaffected by price volatility or shortages, and wind farms can be built in less than two years, which is much faster than most coal or nuclear plants. Wind power can also provide a steady source of income to family farmers and Native American communities whose properties are among the richest potential wind sites.

Solar energy also offers growing potential, especially as technology improvements increase cost-effectiveness. The DOE notes that installation solar photovoltaic devices increased by 33 percent in 2006 over the previous year.[10] The development of solar markets underscores the importance of subsidy policy for catalyzing growth: in 2003, for example, over 80 percent of grid-connected installations in the United States took place in California, where installations are supported by the California Public Utilities Commission self-generation program and the California Energy Commission emerging renewables program.[11] Other renewables with potential for significant future growth include geothermal, small hydrogen power,[12] bio-diesel, and wood energy. Ethanol derived from corn and other plants is serving as a cleaner octane booster in gasoline, but the social and environmental impacts of increased production are significant.[13]

The investment of tax dollars in research and promotion of renewables not only spurs the creation of bigger markets and more cost-effective technologies; it also provides economic and health benefits by reducing air pollution and other environmental problems associated with fossil fuel use.

Establish a Climate and Energy Security Fund Through a Tax on Pollutants

A direct tax on greenhouse gases lies at the center of any effective tax proposal on climate change and energy security. This tax on carbon, methane, and the other greenhouse gases[14] should be imposed as close to the source of production as possible to maximize efficiency. Revenue generated by taxing these greenhouse gases could create a "Climate and Energy Security Fund" that could support investments in efficiency and renewables, as well as relief for those lower-income citizens affected by increasing energy prices and dislocations.

Various studies have shown that pollution taxes, properly targeted, can achieve substantial emissions reductions while helping to pay for themselves, by supporting investments that save money to offset the cost of the pollution tax. In 2002, for example, the Economic Policy Institute (EPI) and Center for a Sustainable Economy released a study that showed how a $50 per ton carbon tax could achieve carbon emission reductions of roughly 10 percent below 1990 levels by 2010, and by 2020 would reduce oil imports by the amount we imported from all members of the Organization of Petroleum Exporting Countries in 2006 *at no net cost to the taxpayer*.[15] That would exceed our targets under the Kyoto Protocol[16] and take us down the road toward independence from foreign oil producers. EPI's basic findings were confirmed in 2004 by the Environmental Protection Agency and Argonne National Laboratory.[17]

The EPI study modeled a set of policies in which 15 percent of the revenues from a carbon "charge" went to income tax reduction, energy efficiency, renewables, and related initiatives. The combined effect of these measures would more than offset the adverse impacts of increased energy prices as consumers would spend less on energy.

A $50 per ton carbon tax, if passed on to consumers, would add about 12.5 cents to a gallon of gasoline.[18]

However, we believe that the United States can achieve similar results at no net cost with *less than half* the $50 per ton carbon tax that the EPI study used if we:

- tax additional pollutants to reflect their health and environmental costs,[19]

- devote more of the proceeds to incentives,

- reduce subsidies for fossil fuels and nuclear power, and

- adopt other policies to encourage energy efficiency and renewables.

The level of tax could be phased in beginning at a low rate for political feasibility and could then be adjusted to avoid the most disruptive price fluctuations as crude oil prices rise and fall and as technology improves.

A $20 per ton fee on carbon would raise about $37 billion annually. The increase in the cost to drivers of about 5 cents per gallon could be offset by reductions in other taxes or tax credits for investments in safe, fuel-efficient tires and other energy-saving measures.

Ensuring that taxpayers break even on increased gas prices would require setting aside about 15 percent of the revenues generated by the fund. However, polls show that people are more likely to support using revenues from pollution taxes to solve environmental problems. Therefore, we recommend dedicating an additional 30 percent of the revenue to promoting efficiency innovations and renewables. This could reduce overall energy bills and further boost climate and energy security. A portion of this amount could go to support greater incentives for the production of plug-in hybrids and electric vehicles, hydrogen produced from renewables, and other efficiencies in transportation.

We could use an additional 15 percent of the revenue to negate the impacts of higher energy prices on low- to moderate-income households initially through reduced-income taxes or subsidies for home heating and cooling systems and increased support for "low-tech" solutions, such as better home insulation.[20] This could also provide jobs in rural and poor areas.

That would still leave 40 percent of the proceeds—nearly $15 billion in new net revenues per year—to administer the program, restore degraded ecosystems that convert carbon dioxide to oxygen, reduce the public debt, and further expedite the transition to a clean economy.

Climate and Energy Security Beyond U.S. Borders

Tax policy at home will have little impact if it doesn't address the global context. One approach would be to set tariffs on imported goods and services to reflect the costs to society when they are produced with dirtier fuel or less sustainable methods than those used for similar domestic goods.[21] The proceeds could be made available to developing countries to reduce pollution and increase energy efficiency and renewables targets.[22] Such green tariffs for aid could become a component in a post-Kyoto international climate change convention.[23] A tariff and loan program is a much gentler precursor to embargoes that are allowed in international law and the General Agreement on Tariffs and Trade (GATT) against those who choose not to use comparable methods of controlling harm to public health or natural resources.[24] Tax and tariff policy could spur faster change if the United States were to impose a tariff that reflects avoided costs due to lower environmental and labor standards in the exporting countries.

Many lessons on the way toward climate and energy security can be learned from Europe, which has been measuring the health costs of air pollution and discussing a pollution tax on imports, as well as partnering with countries outside the European Union (EU) to reduce pollution and promote clean energy.[25] At the national level Sweden has adopted carbon taxes in four stages and is adjusting those to find the most productive balance. Spain, Germany, and Denmark export wind turbines and get a higher percentage of their energy from wind with a much smaller wind resource than exists in the United States. Some Dutch and German houses are steady net generators of energy and income. The United Kingdom is pressing for climate change to head the list of items for international cooperation, and in October 2006, their Head of the Government Economic Service and former World Bank chief economist Sir Nicholas Stern released the Stern Commission Review, which documented the staggering economic costs of inaction on climate change.[26] In November 2006, heads of state of France and Switzerland called for tariffs on imports to offset lax pollution controls and new global carbon taxes to aid in the adaptation to climate change by developing countries.[27]

Outside the EU, Japan leads in vehicle efficiency and production of solar photovoltaics, while Costa Rica saves its forests and coastlines from oil drilling through ecotourism. China recently announced what may be the strictest fuel-efficiency standards, although modern vehicle safety may not yet be incorporated in their requirements. Such positive steps could be rewarded with additional revenue streams from a border carbon tariff at the United States and other borders.

Conclusion: We Can Achieve Climate and Energy Security Now

We can save money and speed up the conversion process to a clean, secure energy future if we impose a carbon tax of roughly $20 per ton, and if we rescind the vast subsidies for non-renewables and tax them to reflect and reduce social and environmental costs beyond climate change. Taxing greenhouse gases and reinvesting the proceeds are the keys to controlling climate change efficiently. Cutting wasteful subsidies that hurt the environment would net billions more in savings while helping to heal ecosystems. Tax reform for climate and energy security represents the best investment we can make in the twenty-first century toward a healthy future for humans and the planet. Pollution taxes are taxes we—and our children's children—can live with.

7

Taxes can promote economic justice for all
Accounting for Racial Inequity

Meizhu Lui

Having wealth—owning more than you owe—is essential to achieving the American dream of economic security and upward mobility. But in the United States in the twenty-first century, access to wealth continues to be shaped by racial inequality: white families are far more likely to realize the American dream than families of other races. The racial wealth gap remains a taxing problem.

For many of us, "income" could just as well be called "outgo." It comes in and then goes out as we pay our monthly expenses. Income is necessary to enable you to survive, but wealth allows you to thrive. Having wealth doesn't mean being rich. It means having a reserve that enables you to weather a health emergency or a period of unemployment, to stop working when you're elderly and not die in poverty, to have some leftover dollars to give your children a jumpstart in life, and to give back to your community.

Meizhu Lui is the executive director of United for a Fair Economy.

So how do people acquire assets in the United States? And why does such an enormous wealth gap exist between white and nonwhite families?

According to the numbers, nonwhites have only fifteen cents for every dollar owned by whites. If you lined up all white families by net worth and picked the one in the middle, that family would have $140,700. For blacks, this median family would have $20,600, and for Latinos, $18,600.[1] Asian Americans are closer, but not equal, to whites in wealth, and Native Americans are clustered with blacks and Latinos. Nonwhite families are far less able to afford homes, to send their children to college, to retire in security, or to pass along an inheritance; disadvantage continues to be passed along from one generation to the next.

An all-too-common, although often unstated, belief about the racial wealth gap is that nonwhites just don't work as hard. And if they don't work as hard, they don't deserve to be equal; and they certainly don't deserve any government assistance, funded by the tax dollars of hard-working white folks! But if hard work is the main route to wealth, then the descendants of slaves should be the wealthiest group in the United States today. And even though U.S. society claims to value hard work, income from wealth (stock dividends, capital gains, and inherited estates) is taxed at a lower rate than income from work.

Taxing Race in U.S. History

Taxes have always been used to redistribute financial resources from one group to another—and for most of U.S.
history, government policy has shifted resources toward
whites and away from nonwhites. Taxes on the Chinese contributed to the wealth divide referred to in a rhyme I heard
as a child: "Ching-chong Chinaman, sitting on fence/trying
to make a dollar out of fifteen cents." During the California
Gold Rush in the mid-1800s, people from all over the world,
including large numbers from both China and Ireland,
flocked to California to find their fortunes. All immigrant
miners faced a tax in California between 1850 and 1855. But
beginning in 1855, the state legislature changed the law so
that the tax fell much more heavily on the Chinese (as well
as a small number of Mexicans) effectively barring them
from mining work since, unlike European immigrants, they
had been made ineligible for citizenship.[2] There were also
special taxes levied on Chinese laundries and other businesses. Taxes on the Chinese accounted for more than
25 percent of California's annual budget between 1850
and 1870.[3]

In the Jim Crow era (which ushered in legally and socially
enforced discrimination against African Americans in the
southern United States beginning in 1876 and lasting
through the mid-1960s), poll taxes levied only on African
Americans prevented them from exercising their constitutional right to vote. The federal government did nothing to

challenge this discriminatory poll tax policy in the southern states for nearly a century. If they had been able to vote, blacks could have won political office and promoted economic opportunity for all, as they were able to do during the brief decade of Reconstruction that followed the Civil War.

Because Native American tribes have the legal status of independent nations, they have been exempted from most federal and state taxes since the founding of the United States. However, just as tribes began to find ways to develop economic assets on their impoverished reservations (such as operating gaming businesses), the rules have been bent: a 1988 law requires tribes to contribute large portions of their revenues to the states in which they are located.[4]

Not only were special taxes levied just on nonwhites, but most tax-funded government programs that helped build and protect wealth were restricted to whites only. The Home Owners' Loan Corporation created by the federal government in 1933 helped homeowners avoid foreclosure during the Depression—but not a single loan out of one million loans went to a black person. The Federal Housing Administration encouraged home ownership by subsidizing mortgages, but red lines were drawn around nonwhite neighborhoods as too risky to warrant loans; instead, tax dollars were intentionally targeted to white suburbs.[5] From 1932 to 1964, out of $120 billion spent on housing subsidies, less than 2 percent went to nonwhites.[6]

Even when the programs were large and allegedly "universal," shares were divided unequally with the largest portion going to white citizens. At the end of World War II, the federal government created asset starter kits for soldiers returning from the war. The GI Bill fully paid for the college tuitions and vocational education costs for 7 million men. But even though this was open to all returning veterans, due to "white only" admission policies in post-secondary schools, few nonwhite veterans were able to benefit, thus widening the racial education gap and limiting the capacity of nonwhites to increase their earnings and savings.

Current Tax Rules Widen the Racial Wealth Gap

But didn't the Civil Rights Movement eliminate racial discrimination and give advantages to nonwhites, so they could catch up?

Civil Rights legislation did help increase employment and income opportunity; however, *asset* inequality was not addressed. And in recent years the tax code has been used to give more breaks to the rich than to help the poor save, a class bias that increases white wealth at the expense of nonwhite families. Between 1995 and 2001, the average nonwhite family saw its net worth fall 7 percent, while an average white family's net worth grew 37 percent.[7]

One way federal tax policy has exacerbated the racial wealth gap is through tax expenditures. "Tax expenditures" give breaks only to certain categories of taxpayers, meaning that the rest of us have to pick up their tab. It's like having your adult son with a high-paid job live at home without paying rent—he's getting a big break, and the rest of the family pays his share. In 2005, the federal government gave up $362 billion dollars in tax expenditures and other tax benefits.

The home mortgage interest deduction, which allows families to subtract the value of their mortgages from their incomes before calculating how much they owe in taxes, is one of the largest tax expenditures, totaling $72.6 billion in 2006. Those who filed tax returns with less than $30,000 in income in 2003 received just 9 percent of deductions for home mortgage interest. By contrast, 36 percent of home mortgage interest deductions were claimed by taxpayers with incomes over $100,000.[8] For homeowners with incomes too low to itemize deductions, there is no tax benefit at all. There are other tax benefits for homeowners including the deduction for property taxes and the exclusion of capital gains on the sale of principle residences. The strong relationship between class and race in the United States, as well as ongoing discrimination in the housing markets, means that home mortgage deductions disproportionately help white families: while three out of four white families are homeowners, only one out of two black families are, and the value of those homes is only one-third of the value of the white home.[9]

Racial differences in access to home ownership translate directly into a wider racial wealth gap. A house is the major asset of many American families, but it tends to be by far the most important asset held by those nonwhite families that have managed to make the jump from renting to owning. In 2001, whites averaged $146,567 in stocks, mutual funds, IRAs, and pensions—more than the $141,769 they held in home ownership. But blacks and Latinos had only $18,082 and $16,797 in stocks and retirement accounts, while they had $45,476 and $53,548 in home equity.[10]

The tax code provides other incentives for asset building in the form of pre-tax deductions, but only those with sufficient wealth are in a position to benefit from them. Deductions for retirement accounts or for college tuition are examples of this problem.

The Tax Code: A "National Wealth Budget"

Tom Shapiro, the co-author with Melvin Oliver of the groundbreaking book *Black Wealth, White Wealth*, calls the tax code "the national wealth budget" because it allocates assets to some groups while excluding others.[11]

But if the bad news is that past and current tax policies favor whites, the good news is that our nation knows how to use tax policy to boost asset-building opportunities and, with enough political will, could use that knowledge to benefit those who have so far been left out.

One tax policy that has helped lift people from poverty is the Earned Income Tax Credit (EITC), which gives low-earning families a cash benefit of about $2,000 a year. The EITC should be expanded to include childless individuals who are working hard and playing by the rules. This year, a new provision allows people to put part of their EITC refund directly into savings accounts; nonwhites are less likely than whites to have bank accounts and therefore may be at greater risk of predatory financial practices such as payday lending, high fees charged to send remittances to families in home countries, and sky-high mortgage or home refinance loans. Becoming "banked" would allow more low-wage workers, who are disproportionately nonwhite, to utilize the same banking services as middle- and upper-class workers, who are disproportionately white. Their savings could be matched by government funds through an expanded Savers Credit program; this would allow faster accumulation of assets to be used for higher education or down payments. Other refundable credits including those cited by Nancy Folbre in chapter 5, such as childcare and elder-care credits, would especially help black, Latino, and Asian women, who are more likely to stay home to care for family members than those in other demographic groups.

Housing tax policies could also better help nonwhite families. Even President Bush's 2005 Advisory Panel on Federal Tax Reform recommended that there be lower limits on the Home Mortgage Interest Deduction (HMID) currently set at $1 million; those owning McMansions do not need a tax break to encourage them to buy one (or two!) of these monstrosities. For low-income homeowners who do not itemize, the mortgage deduction could be made refundable. Some states allow the pre-tax deduction of rent payments on state income taxes; this could also be put into the federal tax code, so as not to penalize those who do not yet have housing assets.

Under the Federal Housing Authority (FHA) tax dollars were targeted to white suburbs up to the 1960s. Today, revenues from lower limits on the HMID could be targeted for affordable housing to inner cities and rural communities that were left out of past programs. The Mayors Task Force on Poverty, Work, and Opportunity suggests a consolidated Jobs Tax Credit to create jobs in high-poverty areas, a program that would help close the racial wealth gap by addressing entrenched class differences.[12]

Race Still Needs Accounting For

The legacy of racially biased tax policies lives on: nonwhites are still "trying to make a dollar out of fifteen cents." Undoing the damage requires understanding the roots of the racial economic hierarchy and focusing national attention on dismantling it. In a color-coded society, "universal" or "colorblind" policies have the intended or unintended consequence of exacerbating or maintaining racial differentials, as in the FHA and GI Bill examples above. Tax policy reform ideas must be examined with a race lens to ensure they do not perpetuate the historical pattern of distributing wealth unequally according to the color line.

Rev. Wyatt Tee Walker, former chief of staff for Dr. Martin Luther King, Jr., recently said, "I heard (Dr. King) say there would never be a major breakthrough in racism until there was a fair distribution of wealth."[13] The tax code can help move us closer to this goal, fulfilling our country's democratic promise of equal opportunity and justice for all.

8

Taxes pay for economic opportunity
The Case for Preserving the Estate Tax

Chuck Collins

The estate tax is an "opportunity-recycling program." It recycles society's investment in wealthy individuals to create opportunities for the next generation.[1]

—Bill Gates Sr.

One of the important moral justifications for progressive taxation is that it recycles common wealth for economic opportunity. By levying a tax on those who have benefited the most from the United State's fertile ground for economic activity, society reclaims wealth to invest in future opportunities.

Much of the debate over taxes is framed in terms of individuals ("it's my money") versus a confiscatory government. In this simplistic framing, we overlook the role that public spending and societal wealth play in enabling individuals to prosper. A closer examination of the estate tax debate contains many lessons relevant not only for

Chuck Collins is a senior scholar at the Institute for Policy Studies defending a tax on inherited wealth, but all forms of progressive taxation.

The Push to Abolish the Estate Tax

Over the past decade, there has been a concerted effort to abolish the federal estate tax, the only U.S. levy on accumulated wealth. Starting in the early 1990s, conservative and anti-tax groups bankrolled a campaign to repeal the so-called death tax. Eighteen super-wealthy families contributed substantially to this effort, including heirs to the Mars candy, Gallo wine, and Walton Wal-Mart family fortunes.[2]

The estate tax is paid when substantial wealth—over $2 million for an individual and $4 million for a couple in 2008—passes from one generation to the next. Originally instituted in 1916, the tax has raised significant amounts of revenue over the decades from the very wealthy. In 2000, Congress voted to repeal the tax, but President Clinton vetoed the legislation, calling it "reckless and irresponsible." He urged Congress to reform the tax by raising the amount of wealth exempted.[3] But the billionaire families bankrolling the effort wouldn't benefit from such a compromise—and held out for an all-or-nothing position.

The package of tax cuts Congress passed in 2001 included a gradual phase-out and elimination of the estate tax in 2010. The law was written to sunset in 2011, at which point the tax will return to its 2001 levels unless Congress takes further action.

Since 2001, congressional tax-cutters have failed to muster the votes required to abolish the tax, largely because of concern about the mushrooming federal deficit and debt. In 2006, congressional conservatives made a bid to couple permanent estate tax reduction with a long overdue boost in the minimum wage in what was ultimately an unsuccessful effort to attract liberal votes.

The public relations effort to abolish the tax propagated a number of myths and distortions. Estate tax opponents misled the public about who actually pays the tax, alleging that it impacts a wide range of households. They claimed that the tax was an unfair form of double taxation, didn't raise much revenue, and heavily burdened small businesses and family farms. They argued that the tax unfairly punished successful people and that there was something unseemly about taxing people at death.

In 2000, several coalitions came together to make the case for responsibly reforming but not abolishing the estate tax. They publicized the fact that only multi-millionaires and billionaires paid the tax, less than 1 percent of all households.[4] They documented that the tax raises substantial revenue, over $30 billion in 2005 and a projected $1 trillion in the ten years between 2012 and 2022. This is the equivalent of a decade of federal spending on housing,

Schedule for Phase-out of Estate Tax

Year	Exclusion Amount	Top Rate
2001*	$675,000	55%
2002	$1 million	50%
2003	$1 million	49%
2004	$1.5 million	48%
2005	$1.5 million	47%
2006	$2 million	46%
2007	$2 million	45%
2008	$2 million	45%
2009	$3.5 million	45%
2010	Repealed	(35%—max. gift tax rate)
2011**	$1 million	55%

*Pre-passage of the Economic Growth and Tax Relief
Reconciliation Act (EGTRRA) of 2001
**After law sunsets

Source: "Tax Policy Issues and Options," no. 2, Dec. 2001, The
Urban Institute. Available at: www.urban.org/
UploadedPDF/310382 taxpolicy 2.pdf.

environmental protection, transportation, and international relations.[5]

Instead of being "double taxation," the bulk of assets subject to estate taxes were found to be appreciated stocks and property, wealth that had never been subject to any taxation.[6] Investigative journalists found that no small farms had been put out of business because of the estate tax and that issues facing small businesses could largely be addressed by raising the amount of wealth exempted by the tax to $2.5 million or $5 million for a couple.[7] The estate tax rate is hardly confiscatory, as its opponents allege. On a $10 million estate, for example, the "effective rate," the actual amount paid after factoring in exemptions, averages 19 percent.[8]

The Case for Preserving a Tax on Inherited Wealth

So the arguments made by estate tax opponents do not hold up to scrutiny. At the same time, there are several important reasons to support the estate tax: it contributes to the progressivity of the overall tax system, boosts charitable giving, and protects our democratic institutions from the power of concentrated wealth.

The estate tax is our nation's most progressive tax. It raises substantial revenue from those most able to pay, deceased multi-millionaires and billionaires. With the federal debt topping $9 trillion, it would be reckless to eliminate a tax that will bring in more than $1 trillion over the next decade and grow in the decades to come.[9] Eliminating the tax either shifts the tax burden onto less affluent taxpayers, forces tax cuts on services, or leaves unreasonable amounts of debt for the next generation.

The estate tax is a tremendous incentive for wealthy people to give to charity. Because wealthy people can reduce their estate taxes dollar for dollar by giving to charity, many chose to create foundations or direct contributions to hospitals, universities, and arts and culture. Many of these donations might be made in the absence of an estate tax. But research shows that without the incentive of the estate tax, there would be a 22 to 37 percent decline in charitable bequests. In 2007, this would translate into $10–13 billion less flowing to the charitable sector.[10]

The estate tax protects our democracy by putting a break on the build-up of concentrated wealth and power. The estate tax was instituted in response to the excessive inequality of the Gilded Age, 1890–1915. At the turn of the century, the public widely believed this concentration of wealth could corrupt the fragile U.S. experiment in democratic self-governance.[11] As Supreme Court Justice Louis Brandeis is widely quoted as saying, "We can have concentrated wealth in the hands of a few or democracy—but we cannot have both." We are now living through our second Gilded Age, as wealth concentration has reached extreme levels. The richest 1 percent of households now owns more than 34.3 percent of all private wealth and 42.2 percent of financial assets.[12]

A century ago, President Theodore Roosevelt supported the Sixteenth Amendment to allow for income and estate taxes. Roosevelt argued, "Such taxation should, of course, be aimed merely at the inheritance or transmission in their entirety of those fortunes swollen beyond all healthy limits.[13] Industrialist Andrew Carnegie, one of the richest men in the country, testified in favor of the creation of a federal inheritance tax. In *The Gospel of Wealth*, Carnegie wrote of the estate tax:

> Of all forms of taxation this seems the wisest. Men who continue hoarding great sums all their lives, the proper use of which for public ends would work good to the community from which it chiefly came, should be made to feel that the community, in the form of the State, cannot thus be deprived of its proper share.[14]

Carnegie also suggested that too much inherited wealth is bad for the heirs and heiresses. Leaving wealth to descendents, in Carnegie's opinion, was "most injudicious" and deadening to the development of children's talents and energies. "I would as soon leave to my son a curse as the almighty dollar," wrote Carnegie. A parent leaving wealth to a child should admit that it is "not the welfare of the children, but family pride, which inspires these legacies."[15]

In the last few years, advocates of retaining the estate tax have labeled it "the Paris Hilton tax," shifting the debate to focus on "undeserving" heirs and heiresses who did nothing to create the wealth, rather than the mythological farmers and small business owners.

A Wealth Recycling Program

The strongest affirmative case for a tax on inherited wealth lies in the fact that it enables society to recapture its investment in individuals and recycle it for future generations. The debate over the estate tax has focused too much on the inconvenience to wealthy taxpayers, overlooking the ways that government spending creates opportunities for individuals to develop their gifts and contribute to society.

In 2001, more than 2,500 multi-millionaires and billionaires signed a public petition, sponsored by Responsible Wealth, a national network of affluent citizens concerned about growing inequality in the United States, in favor of retaining the estate tax.[16] This "billionaire backlash," as *Newsweek* called it, garnered enormous media attention and began to shift the debate about the rationale for retaining the tax. Super-investor Warren Buffett argued in the *New York Times* that repealing the estate tax would undermine meritocracy and "be a terrible mistake" comparable to "choosing the 2020 Olympic team by picking the eldest sons of the gold-medal winners in the 2000 Olympics."[17]

High net worth individuals, when interviewed about their support for wealth taxation, described the ways that society helped them become wealthy—and their obligation to "give back" in the form of taxation and charitable giving. One prosperous entrepreneur, Martin Rothenberg, explained in a statement, "I hope taxes on my estate will help fund the kind of programs that benefited me and others from humble backgrounds—a good education, money for research, and targeted investments in poor communities—to help bring opportunity to all Americans."[18]

These responsible wealthy recognize that they have bene-fited enormously from society's investments in scientific and technological research, public infrastructure, and other forms of socially owned wealth. Through our taxpayer-funded investments, the United States has created a unique and fertile ground for private enterprise. This is why Bill Gates Sr., the father of the founder of Microsoft, refers to the estate tax as the "gratitude tax." Gates writes that wealthy individuals:

> have made good use of their "American inheritance," including our accumulated scientific heritage and nat-ural bounty. They have harvested plenty from our soci-ety's investments in technology and our remarkable

system of property laws and regulated markets. Without this inheritance, they frankly wouldn't have succeeded in quite the same way.[19]

Abolishing the estate tax would de-fund this "opportunity-recycling program"

Gates Sr. and some Responsible Wealth members share a common memory. They received the GI Bill or other subsidies for housing, education, or small business after World War II. Society made a substantial investment in this "greatest generation," and many of them feel grateful and obliged to pass on the gift.

These "gratitude" stories stand in marked contrast to the "I did it alone" narratives that you hear from proponents of abolishing the estate tax and all forms of progressive taxation. Rather than "punishing successful people," progressive taxation recognizes that some individuals have disproportionately benefited from society's investments and have a special obligation to pay them back.

There is a practical as well as a moral argument to be made for recycling opportunity by taxing wealth: it is a crucial foundation for generating future wealth. The myth of a self-made millionaire or billionaire ignores this foundation. While individual effort and creativity clearly matter, they fail to explain or justify the great accumulations of private wealth that have occurred in the last several decades.

Individual wealth depends on a healthy and robust common wealth, or "commons." This largely invisible commons includes, in the words of social entrepreneur Peter Barnes, "the gifts of nature, plus the gifts of society that we share and inherit together—and that we have an obligation to pass onto our heirs, undiminished and more or less equally."[20]

The commons includes our ecological bounty (water, air, oceans, soil, seeds). One reason we pay taxes is to protect and preserve this ecological commons that is the source of life and our future sustenance. The private market, bolstered by our myth of individual achievement, tends to undervalue this and other taxpayer-funded sources of common social wealth, such as our legal system and property law protection, including intellectual property; public investments in science and technology; public education; grants to universities and colleges; the broadcast spectrum, the Internet and spin-off commons like Wikipedia; and shared cultural assets. Any contribution of present-day individuals is a cherry on the top of gigantic banana split.

We are dangerously diminishing and disinvesting the commons that was built for us. The push to limit taxes has led to massive deficits. Just look at the state of the nation's roads, bridges, and rail infrastructures as an example. On behalf of our children, we have a self-interested stake, as well as a civic obligation, in preserving a healthy commons that recycles economic opportunity.

Drawing in part on this rationale, Washington State voters chose in a November 2006 ballot initiative to retain their estate tax by substantial margins. Revenue from the state's tax is dedicated to an Education Legacy Trust Fund that in 2005 spent $100 million to reduce K–12 class size and provide college scholarships for working-class students. This is an excellent example of using estate tax revenue to expand and recycle opportunity, a design we should consider for the federal estate tax.

If we don't see the commons, give it status, and identify the substantial gifts that each of us receive, we will impoverish ourselves by continuing to live by the myth of individual achievement. If we recognize the substantial common inheritance that we each receive, by virtue of living and doing business in the United States, we can appreciate the obligation we have to pass on the gift, through progressive taxes, charitable giving, and community involvement. When we understand the role of the commons in individual wealth creation, we understand the necessity of an estate tax.

9

Taxes are good for business
Supporting People-Centered, Community-Oriented Companies

John Abrams and Greg LeRoy

From a corporate perspective, paying taxes is not just a legal obligation; it's a matter of self-interest. Taxes, when appropriately applied, enable many things that help businesses, but which no company by itself could afford to create, such as skilled labor, efficient infrastructure, public health, and civil justice.

Of course, paying into a system that has allowed you to prosper can also be seen as a civic duty. As described by Chuck Collins in chapter 8, business leaders like Bill Gates Sr. and Warren Buffett have defended the federal estate tax by pointing out that their wealth was enabled in part by public goods and that therefore it is appropriate that inherited wealth be taxed. Says Buffett, "If you stick me down in the middle of Bangladesh or Peru or someplace, you'll find out how much this talent is going to produce in the wrong kind of soil. I will be struggling thirty years later. I work in a

John Abrams is co-founder and CEO of South Mountain Company. Greg LeRoy founded and directs Good Jobs First.

market system that happens to reward what I do very well—disproportionately well."[1] He's clear about his obligation to help the society that helps him.

To be sure, most business people want taxes to be as low as possible and government to be efficient. But for business leaders thinking long term, the more important issue is not how much we pay in taxes (business tax burdens in the United States have been declining for decades and are nearly the lowest among developed nations) but rather how our taxes are used. We want our taxes to be fair, predictable, and effectively spent. We especially want our taxes to be spent for those things we believe are important.

Although the more ideological business associations fixate simply on cutting taxes, business leaders in the United States in the twenty-first century are hardly of one mind about the taxes we pay and the uses we make of tax revenue. Increasingly, some businesses see their taxes (and the public services they support) as not just a self-interested investment and civic duty, but also as a creative tool that can complement their business strategy, project their values, and strengthen their communities.

By supporting goals like broadening the ownership of a company, providing more home ownership and more affordable housing, or supporting energy efficiency and renewable energy, tax policies can become incentives for a better world, as well as an improved business climate.

Of course, what a better world looks like depends on your

perspective. Some large and mobile corporations, with no attachments to a particular place, can easily view taxes as an abstraction, just one more cost to be reduced. For locally owned companies, and for larger companies that consciously decide to embrace a people-centered, community-oriented business philosophy, taxes are an investment in the future, like workforce training or new equipment.

Workforce Housing in a Bubble Market

The housing market offers a key example of how tax policy could be used more effectively to support business goals that enhance the public good. Rising housing prices have begun to affect many U.S. markets, especially since the late 1990s, when the increase in home prices far exceeded overall inflation in many states. Many low- and middle-income families have been displaced, often forced to move further away from their jobs.

Businesses, including large employers and chambers of commerce, around the country are responding by supporting local initiatives for affordable housing and "workforce" housing.[2] Businesses can also directly support expanded housing options for their employees. For example, the design/build firm South Mountain Company (SMC—founded and run by John Abrams) uses a feature of the tax code, deductions for charitable donations, to add to the affordable housing stock in its Martha's Vineyard location, a place known as an upscale resort island where the wealthy vacation and make second homes. Long-term gentrification has cost many year-round residents their access to affordable rental housing and made home ownership ever more difficult. In light of the problems this presented both to employees and to the community as a whole, the SMC decided to use a creative tax strategy to help preserve affordable housing for the Vineyard's working families. When someone wants to demolish an older home to make way for a new structure, which happens with increasing frequency as property values skyrocket, they instead donate the house to the nonprofit Island Affordable Housing Fund, getting a tax deduction for its value. They give the fund a check for 100 percent of their anticipated tax savings for itemizing the donation. They save demolition and removal costs, and the SMC gets a home and cash to be able to move it, bring it up to code, and sell it affordably by lottery to qualified residents. The homes are deed restricted to ensure they will remain affordable forever.

Leveraging federal and state income tax deductions is not the whole story. SMC, like other Vineyard property owners, also pays a 3 percent local property tax surcharge on its headquarters building; this surcharge supports programs for affordable housing and historic preservation. The company would pay more if the rate was raised, and the island would be well served. SMC worked hard to convince others that taxing themselves to create affordable housing is an essential aspect of preservation of our community and a prosperous economy. The voters responded, and now all property owners pay this surcharge. As a result of this self-imposed community enhancement tax, businesses and their employees can enjoy a more stable and more profitable economic environment.

Workforce Development: The Demographic Imperative

While progress has been made in housing, other issues important to both businesses and communities continue to get short shrift. Creating the political will to connect long-term self-interest with short-term investments in services and programs funded by higher taxes is not easy. One of the clearest examples of a collective failure to make this connection has been in education and workforce development. The 76 million-member Baby Boom generation is aging, and the bulge of Boomer retirements that will begin in 2008 will trigger a long-term skilled labor shortage. Labor economists debate the severity, but many trade associations are already reporting shortages in industries such as healthcare, engineering, teaching, and transportation.

In the last two decades of the twentieth century, the number of U.S. residents in their prime work years—age 25 to 54—grew by 35 million (as Boomers came of age). In the first two decades of the twenty-first century, the net growth in prime-age workers will be only 3 million, as

Boomers retire and are succeeded by the much smaller Gen X and Echo Boom cohorts.

The prosperous metro areas of the twenty-first century will be those that are best at growing and attracting young, smart workers. Every dollar we spend in the name of economic development should deliver more skilled labor. But perversely, some of the most lucrative tax breaks given to "improve the business climate" actually undermine schools.

The stakes are high. Public schools are the largest beneficiaries of local property and sales taxes, and the quality of local schools is critical to an area's economic competitiveness. When companies shop for places to relocate or expand, the number one issue is finding an adequate supply of skilled labor, which requires good schools that will graduate skilled future workers and attract talented employees from other areas as well.

American families care about their schools. Those who can routinely move into areas with higher housing costs to gain access to better schools. And they support bond issues for public schools at a greater rate than they do other services, except healthcare. They do this despite the fact that families don't get a ten-year holiday on their property tax for moving into their preferred school district; companies, on the other hand, often do.

So when companies seek long-term property tax abatements (and various other exemptions) and when localities grant them in the name of promoting a "good business climate," they are actually eroding their long-term competitive edge. By undermining funding for public schools, they are reducing the community's ability to attract good talent. Given the graying of America, such disinvestment is perilously shortsighted. The business community should recognize this and be willing to pay the necessary local taxes as a long-term investment in tomorrow's workforce.

The Infrastructure Deficit: A Productivity and Public Health Time Bomb?

Another good reason for paying taxes is our nation's yawning infrastructure deficit and the harm it may inflict on our productivity and public health. The extreme example, of course, is the levies in New Orleans, but they are hardly an isolated case. The American Society of Civil Engineers grades our various infrastructure systems every couple of years, and the grades have been going steadily down, so that they are now a cumulative D.

Traffic congestion reduces productivity and wastes fuel to the tune of $67.5 billion per year. More than one-fourth of the nation's bridges are structurally deficient or functionally obsolete, so they cannot handle all vehicles. Transit spending is one-half what it needs to be just to maintain the systems. Three out of four school buildings are inadequate; the cumulative rebuilding deficit is $127 billion.

Drinking-water systems are mostly reliable but aging; they need $11 billion a year more than they are getting in upgrades and rehab to comply with federal rules. Waste-water systems are in such bad shape that we risk losing all of the gains made in surface water purity since the 1972 Clean Water Act.

Investment in power transmission systems has declined so badly that the U.S. Department of Energy estimates that the nation's power grid needs $50 billion worth of modernization. Half the locks on our inland waterways are older than the fifty years they were designed to last. Almost 2,600 dams are now deemed unsafe, and more than 10,000 dams are upstream from development, meaning their collapse would inflict casualties.

Overall, the civil engineers estimate that to renew our infrastructure will cost us $1.6 trillion. Tax reduction movements undermine these systems even more; reducing taxes puts off for tomorrow what needs to be done today.

The Growing Divide Between Locally Owned Businesses and Absentees

So if businesses benefit from socially responsible programs funded by adequate taxes, why aren't all businesses on board? And what differentiates firms that align their self-interest with the long-term health of their communities from those that do not? In her new book, *Big-Box Swindle*, Stacy Mitchell summarizes a small but startling body of sociological literature on how monopolism erodes public well-being.[3] From a study performed—and then suppressed—by the U.S. Department of Agriculture in the 1940s up through contemporary academic work, research has repeatedly found that communities dominated by large businesses are less healthy than those that still retain a collection of smaller, locally owned companies and other local institutions. The affected areas range from public health (birth weights to murder rates) to economics (income inequality and unemployment) to voting turnout rates and other kinds of civic participation.

The data suggest that communities that are characterized by local entrepreneurial leadership are broadly healthier. When the economic ecosystem enables local talent to play a strong role—when people who are deeply connected to the community are influential—everyone benefits.

Local entrepreneurs, unlike multi-nationals, are much more likely to benefit from local tax dollars and to feel the negative impact of local tax cuts or breaks. In contrast to a firm like Wal-Mart, which has sought and received more than $1 billion in "economic development" subsidies, local merchants are more likely to incorporate the connection between taxes and services into business location and hiring decisions. A locally rooted business person would realize, for example, that if she received a property tax abatement, the school attended by her children and those of her customers would receive correspondingly less funding. An executive in Bentonville in charge of shaving taxes would not have the same concern.

On taxes and many other issues—such as globalization, economic inequality, and suburban sprawl—locally owned businesses have a more immediate bottom-line incentive to care about their communities. And for small, place-based businesses, there is far more opportunity to impact local taxes and the programs they support than those at the state and federal level, both in degree and application. Local businesses can work for taxes that levy burdens on things we don't want (like more carbon in the atmosphere) rather than things we do want (like more income).

Taxes shouldn't be thought of as an abstraction that can be described by demagogic sound bites. They are what we use to build strong, stable prosperous communities. If we take an active role in determining the kind of taxes we pay and how they are used, we can make a better business climate, and a better world, too.

10

Taxes fuel democracy
Funding Institutions That Champion
Democratic Participation

**Stuart Comstock-Gay, Michael Lipsky, Miles
Rapoport, and Stephanie Greenwood**

Democracy costs money. Specifically, it costs *public*
money—tax dollars collected from everyone to support institutions that benefit everyone. Any other funding mechanism simply wouldn't work. Financing elections through
poll taxes, for example, or charging user fees for contract
enforcement or education would automatically produce
undemocratic results. Only those with the ability to pay
would have access to the political process and would be
able to dominate its key institutions. The central promise
of democratic government—that citizens can exert political
influence regardless of their economic or social status—
would break down.

Most people who believe in the ideal of democracy would
recoil from a system in which only those with sufficient

Stuart Comstock-Gay is the director of Dēmos's Democracy Program.
Michael Lipsky is a senior program director at Dēmos. Miles Rapoport is
the president of Dēmos.

private means had the chance to make political decisions that affect everyone. But in recent years the United States has drifted troublingly close to this state of affairs.

Supreme Court Justice Oliver Wendell Holmes Jr. wrote "Taxes are what we pay for civilized society" in 1927, during a period of American history characterized by problems that are familiar today, including great inequality and excessive influence of money in politics.[1] The case behind his famous statement sheds interesting light on our present-day tax debate. He was arguing (in a dissenting opinion) that a foreign insurance company had to pay a disputed tax, because the government used tax money in part to offer protection to the insured goods traveling through its territory. The tax was constitutional because those who benefit from the protection of the government may be taxed to defray the costs of such protection—even if they themselves can't see the benefit they reap from paying into the system.

Then and now, the benefits provided by tax-funded democratic institutions can be hard to see, in part because so often they are indirect and diffuse. But that does not make those benefits any less real—or less costly. Ironically, when taxes work well, they fund an environment in which the problems that might make us appreciate the need for a stronger public sector do not arise. This can make us forgetful about the role taxes play in supporting institutions vital to our individual and collective well-being. Rather than a bill gladly paid for the privilege of living in a decent society, taxes have come to be regarded—with a lot of help from a concerted anti-government movement embraced by many political figures—as a drain on productive activity that distorts incentives to work and supports a wasteful government bureaucracy. This shift in perception has extremely serious consequences for our ability to fund the institutions that keep government representative and accountable to all citizens.

Democracy on the Cheap?

Anti-tax ideology has become so pervasive that many people advocate reducing government expenditures without confronting the impact of those reductions on critical democratic institutions. These institutions can be grouped into two basic categories: those that allow all citizens, regardless of socioeconomic status, a political voice; and those that ensure that the mechanics of democratic activity, particularly the act of voting itself, function well enough to produce results in which the public can have confidence.

Recent political and economic trends, particularly widespread tax revolts accompanied by persistent resistance to any tax increases, have had a deteriorating impact on both categories. As a result, we risk running what might be called a "democracy deficit." By chronically underfunding the institutions necessary to democratic participation, we are building up a debt that must be paid with interest by future generations, or, if left unpaid, that will erode the credibility of the country's most basic democratic claims.[2]

Underinvesting in access to political participation

Tax revolts have taken an especially troubling toll on our ability to mobilize support for institutions that make meaningful democratic participation possible for all citizens, regardless of socioeconomic status. These include good public schools and public universities, public policies such as health insurance, quality childcare that is necessary for some parents to participate in the labor force, and minimal wage supports that help people obtain economic resources sufficient to have a stake in society despite persistent economic and social divisions.

Taxing ourselves to fund access to democratic participation for all is much more difficult and controversial than paying the public cost of basic rights. Divisions of race and class that simmer beneath most debates on taxes—particularly when it comes to school financing or social welfare programs—drive wedges between our democratic ideals and the reality in which we live by pitting cities and suburbs, rich and poor, old-time residents and newcomers against each other in an unbalanced competition over scarce resources. Failures to support public policies responsive to the needs of the most vulnerable, and efforts to withdraw public resources from the so-called undeserving (primarily low-income residents and immigrants) have undermined political access in communities where it is particularly needed.

Challenging as it is, successfully funding institutions that give political voice to the economically disenfranchised would actually solve only part of the problem. A comprehensive approach would also prevent the wealthy from buying undue political influence. The influence of money in politics may be the single greatest challenge to American democracy. And it seems to defy correction because the people who would have to make the decisions to reform the system are its current beneficiaries.

In the United States, although every voter has only one vote, individuals with greater financial resources have more say simply because they have more money. "Organized money," the writer Gore Vidal has observed, "has long since replaced organized people as the author of our politics."[3] This is particularly true when it comes to electoral campaigns, where money can shape political outcomes by buying media advertisements, hiring expert staff, or bankrolling sophisticated, selective voter turnout operations.

Money has such influence in election campaigns primarily because they are funded privately rather than publicly. The consequences for democracy are substantial. Our candidates are less varied, and their positions cannot stray far from the line approved by donors. So long as access to money is a prerequisite to electoral participation, minority communities and the nonwealthy will be denied candidates who fully represent them. Some years ago, John Bonifaz and Jamie Raskin termed this problem the "wealth primary." As a result of the wealth primary, they observed, "American democracy is seeing fewer and fewer citizens with ordinary jobs and ordinary salaries going into politics, and almost none winning. And if you are poor, you can just about forget it."[4]

Candidates who spend the most money win. In the 2004 races for state legislatures, for example, the candidate who spent the most money won 87 percent of the time. In congressional elections that year, candidates who spent the most money for a seat in the House of Representatives won virtually all of the time (97 percent). Less than 1 percent of the population makes financial contributions over $200 to candidates for federal office. These contributions represent the vast majority of funds that candidates receive from individuals. Of this tiny fraction of the population, seven out of eight have household incomes of $100,000 or more, 70 percent are male, and 96 percent are white. Personal wealth of candidates is also a factor in our elections. While only one in 125 Americans are millionaires (as of July 2004), in the last Congress at least 45 percent of U.S. Senators and 24 percent of U.S. House members were millionaires.[5]

The privatization of responsibility for raising money for elections not only skews the population of people who run for office and win. It also poisons the representative's job. Time is the most valuable and scarce asset officeholders have, and they give it away to contributors as a matter of course and self-preservation. The demands on the office-holder to raise money for the next campaign are so great that legislators must spend most of their time raising money—time that could be better spent learning about the issues or interacting with a wide range of constituents. To raise adequate funds for an average race for the House of Representatives, members must raise $2,000 every day they are in office. Members of Congress regularly bemoan the emphasis they must place on raising money and how much they resent this distraction from their duties.

So far, seeking to limit campaign contributions has met with limited success. A more comprehensive approach would be to pay for campaigning *entirely or mostly with tax dollars*. At a stroke such a measure would increase the diversity and broaden the pool of candidates who run for office, increase the chances that candidates with new ideas would come forward and run meaningful campaigns, and improve the working conditions of elected officials, leaving them with more time to do the work of government.

Models for public campaign financing are readily available. Maine, Arizona, and Connecticut all currently fund state elections with public dollars. New Jersey, New Mexico, and North Carolina provide full public financing for some elections. Countries no less democratic than the

United States, such as Australia, Sweden, the Netherlands, France, Italy, and Germany, all provide some form of public support. And many countries, including Great Britain and Canada, provide free airtime, reducing candidates' campaign costs.

Underinvesting in election administration

The second set of institutions necessary to a healthy democracy often gets less attention: they support the mechanics of the electoral system, particularly the hallmark activity of democratic participation—voting. Although fundamental law guarantees the right to vote, socioeconomic status significantly determines a given individual's access to voting procedures and the likelihood of voting. But factors that might seem more mundane also play a key role in determining people's ability to participate in elections: the presence of a working, adequately staffed voting machine; ease of ability to register; absence of barriers such as onerous identification requirements or felon disenfranchisement laws.[6]

The debacle of the 2000 presidential election awakened large numbers of Americans to a realization that elections only seemed to run on autopilot. Deep down there were flaws in registration processes and the administration of elections—flaws serious enough to jeopardize our confidence in the entire democratic process. In response, Congress passed the Help Americans Vote Act (HAVA), which authorized $3.9 billion for election improvements. With guidance from the newly created Election Assistance Commission, the money was to be spent by states and localities to make the necessary corrections to their election machinery.

But the elections of 2004 and 2006 showed that the problems have hardly been solved. Long lines, equipment malfunctions, lack of sufficient machines and poorly trained poll workers continue to plague our national "Day of Decision." The newest voting booth technology continues to suffer from security and reliability problems, prompting several state governors to demand machines that generate paper trails. Only now, as we try radically to upgrade our election machinery, do we realize the price we pay for running elections on nickels and dimes.

HAVA funding also did not succeed in addressing the array of problems stemming from the "crazy-quilt" nature of our election administration system. There are roughly 3,000 different jurisdictions—states, counties, and municipalities—that have responsibility for deciding what poll workers will be paid and how they are trained, what kinds of machines to buy, what kind of list management to undertake, what standards will be used to count votes, and how recounts and controversies will be settled. Many states run elections on the basis of lists that are maintained by county or municipal officials on separate systems that cannot communicate with one another. Rules for "purging" voters are often unclear, leading to uncertainty over reliability of election lists. Errors resulting from voters having the same or similar names, and from data entry problems, cause large-scale confusion and sometimes result in eligible voters being turned away from the polls. Although HAVA required states to have clean, statewide computerized lists by January of 2006, only very few states met the standard.

To make matters worse, many of the officials who make election administration decisions have at the same time both governmental and partisan campaign responsibilities.[7] This contradiction is so egregious that former President Jimmy Carter has said that the Carter Center, if asked to do so, would not be able to send election observers to the United States as it does to other countries because the U.S. does not meet international standards for electoral democracy.

The problems undermining our electoral system are all preventable—for a price. And once again the nature of the problems means that this price must be paid in tax dollars rather than private donations or fees. We need a publicly funded election system with adequate resources to support reliable equipment, accurate, accessible registration lists and well-trained polling staff. The system also requires a publicly funded national election agency with enough resources to monitor, conduct research, and set clear national standards for voting procedures.

Taxing ourselves at a level sufficient to fund the institutions that support democratic participation, including access to political influence and an electoral system in which the public can have confidence, won't be cheap. But it should be seen as an essential investment by people across the political spectrum who care about fair, representative government. In many ways, the democratic character of our government depends on a robust, progressive tax system. Our ability to realize the promise of American democracy depends upon widespread recognition that we must pay the costs of doing so.

Conclusion
Changing the Tax Debate

Stephanie Greenwood

Any thoughtful debate about taxes raises two questions: (1) What kind of society do we want? and (2) How are we going to pay for it? These questions are not neutral. They involve deeply held beliefs and zero-sum conflicts over the public resources that support the foundation of decent private lives. These include: a relatively stable, secure environment, legal protections and recourse for violations of fundamental rights, institutions that allow some measure of opportunity and mobility, and responsive government representation. Decisions about how to allocate these resources call up tensions between individual self-interest (how do I and my family benefit?) and collective self-interest (how can we fund a system that serves our social needs and remains roughly compatible with our normative ideals?).

The contributors to this collection argue that addressing the gap between the society we've paid for and the society we want will require a major reframing of our national debate on taxes.

Such a change is not without precedent; beliefs about the role taxes should play in the United States have transformed dramatically over the last century. The Great Depression brought about a seismic shift in public opinion and policy, discrediting the laissez-faire approach of a small, noninterventionist government that had prevailed from the country's founding through the 1920s and creating a series of massive tax-funded employment and social security programs. The legacy of the New Deal continues to affect public perceptions of government as responsible for cushioning citizens against the risks of a capitalist market economy.

Following World War II, New Deal programs such as the GI Bill paved the way for President Lyndon B. Johnson's Great Society, which sought to extend the benefits of the postwar economy to everyone, particularly the urban poor. These efforts grew from the awareness that meaningful participation in the political process required some measure of economic and social security—and that programs for achieving this democratic prerequisite could and should and be funded through progressive taxes. Although there was plenty of opposition, especially to tax-funded programs targeted at low-income black and immigrant communities, there was also broad public consensus that the system itself should be progressive and that most citizens benefited from that progressivity.

The policies of the mid-twentieth century succeeded in

lifting many Americans to middle-class status while leaving behind large pockets of continued deprivation. Nevertheless, federal programs increasingly came to be seen as transfers of cash from the industrious middle class to the undeserving poor. Support grew for tax revolts that sought to limit the scope of government activity, especially when it involved redistribution down the income ladder. During the Reagan administration, the notion of "trickle-down economics" gained official sanction, and tax revolts began to grow in strength, influence, and institutional sponsorship, with grassroots campaigns lobbying for tax reduction and think tanks and organizations producing sophisticated policy materials on the ills of big government.

These efforts found their institutional embodiment in 1986 when anti-tax advocate Grover Norquist founded Americans for Tax Reform, a group dedicated to ensuring that politicians sign and abide by a pledge to oppose all tax increases (and at the federal level to oppose decreases to tax breaks). Signing the Pledge has become a virtual prerequisite for most Republicans and for many Democrats running in Republican districts. Norquist is widely credited for bringing big business interests into coalition with grassroots conservatives on an anti-tax platform and most recently for orchestrating political support for the Bush tax cuts in pursuit of his aspiration "to get [government] down to the size where we can drown it in the bathtub."[1]

Results at the polls suggest that the anti-tax message finds a receptive audience among middle- and working-class Americans as well as wealthy beneficiaries. The large, regressive tax cuts of 2001 and 2002, for example, enjoyed broad popular support, even among people that recognized and disapproved of increasing economic inequality, many of whom would themselves be hurt by the cuts. According to political scientist Larry Bartels, this puzzle may be explained in part by a certain amount of confusion in the public mind about the consequences of the tax cuts: "[M]ost Americans supported tax cuts not because they were indifferent to economic inequality, but because they largely failed to connect inequality and public policy."[2]

But popular support for tax cuts is only part of the story—and not an entirely straightforward part. While survey respondents report that they support large tax cuts, they also express strong support for large, tax-funded programs. According to researchers Jacob Hacker and Paul Pierson, "[V]oters consistently saw tax cuts as a lower priority than plausible alternative uses of the forecasted surpluses," such as shoring up Social Security or Medicaid.[3]

Popular support for tax cuts—and aggressive political organizing to make that support salient to politicians—no doubt plays a role in their legislative success. But it may be even more important that the wealthy, to whose interests politicians tend to be most responsive, today generally don't have much of a stake in the health of the public sphere. As a result of large and growing economic inequality, those at the top are in a position to withdraw their resources from society in what Robert Reich has called the "secession of the successful."[4] As Reich notes, the withdrawal extends even to charitable giving, as most donations from the wealthy go to support institutions such as private universities and arts organizations primarily used by the wealthy themselves. This "secession" is visible in the increasing prevalence of the private provision of healthcare, childcare, and education—even parks and police. A more subtle and devastating withdrawal has also taken place at the neighborhood level, as local land use and zoning laws create exclusive wealthy suburban enclaves that reserve the best public facilities only for those that can afford to buy in. And, as Meizhu Lui points out, even those that can afford to buy in are sometimes unfairly excluded on the basis of race or ethnic origin.

The combined effect of popular support for regressive tax cuts and the withdrawal of the wealthy from "the commons," discussed by Chuck Collins, has created a situation in which revenues no longer fund an adequate level of services and access to opportunity for all the country's inhabitants. The squeeze on budgets has been particularly painful at the state level, as anti-tax "successes" constrain spending on important public services and institutions. The cuts appear to be having a serious impact: as noted by Stan Karp, California's Proposition 13 drastically limited property tax increases beginning in 1978, resulting in large reductions in spending on public schools. The change in funding coincided with a rapid drop in student achievement. From one of the top performing school systems in the country, California has seen its students' scores in reading and math plummet to the third lowest in the nation, above only Louisiana and Mississippi.[5]

Parallel stories that link tax revolts to reduced spending to deteriorating quality of life for working- and middle-class Americans can be told about healthcare, housing, childcare, and other social necessities, as well as more fundamental, less tangible goods, such as access to meaningful democratic participation. We are in the midst of a strange moment in U.S. tax history, one in which benefits accrue to an increasingly small fraction of the population, while the rest of us pay into a system that moves further and further away from meeting our needs.

Realigning the tax system with our social needs and priorities would involve adopting many of the reforms suggested in this book, including better funding for public schools, more attention to the needs of children and families, support for a more functional electoral system, and strategic use of tax policy to further goals such as climate-change mitigation support for a healthy business environment and redressing the racial wealth gap. In some cases, these reforms require more taxes, but in others they simply require smarter, better-targeted, more fairly collected taxes. All of them involve renouncing knee-jerk, anti-tax ideology in favor of a system that supports a healthy society, one in which people all across the income spectrum participate and feel a stake.

Successful reform means fundamentally changing the debate about taxes, starting with the question of how best to fund the kind of society we want, as a matter of self-interest, civic pride, and, as Susan Pace Hamill reminds us, as a matter of conscience. This vision must then be reconciled with some harsh budgetary realities: the funding pool is limited, self-interest is generally a more powerful force than social interest, and difficult trade-offs among competing priorities must be made.

Successful tax reform also needs to recognize the valid criticisms of tax revolters: today's tax system may be inadequate to our needs, but it can also fairly be accused of wasting vast sums through overwhelming complexity and inefficiency. A strong case for progressive tax reform must tackle these criticisms head-on and include provisions to simplify and streamline collections.

Changing the national debate on taxes also means creating enough general awareness and education about the relationship between taxes and services to breaks through the formidable "simplicity constraint" that confounds our responses to harmful tax cuts. We would also need to overcome a certain reluctance many of us have to engage with an issue that can seem boring and arcane on the one hand and contentious and frustrating on the other.

Finally, in a political moment when the country is funding activities that many citizens find troubling, it seems fair to ask whether fighting to increase the capacity of the government through a stronger, more progressive tax system is even a good idea. When I first told a friend that I would be editing a book on ten excellent reasons to pay taxes, he laughed and said, "Make sure you mention prisoner abuse in foreign detention centers and federal emergency response to hurricanes." He had a point. Several books could easily be published on the subject of why a person might *not* want to pay taxes, either for ethical reasons, in the tradition of Thoreau, despair at bureaucratic mismanagement and neglect, or simply personal financial difficulty imposed by today's uncertain and inequitable economy.

But withdrawing from the field on taxes means offering silent support to the notion that paying for a healthy society is not a collective responsibility—that those who can should stay behind privately fortified walls using privately funded services and those who can't should try to make it on their own. As more and more U.S. residents find themselves outside those walls, unable to sustain a secure and prosperous life for themselves and their children, the individualist position becomes increasingly untenable and the opportunity to engage in a broad, thoughtful debate on the role of taxes in society grows.

The chapters in this book offer a jumping-off point for this urgently needed change in the tax debate. They invite us to put our minds where our money is and to engage in the arduous, long-term process of wrestling the tax system into a more efficient and more equitable force for the social good.

Notes

Introduction

1.   Edmund Burke, *Select Works of Edmund Burke,* vol. 2: *Reflections on the Revolution in France* (1790), The Online Library of Liberty, Classics in the History of Liberty. Available at: http://oll.libertyfund.org/Texts/LFBooks/Burke0061/SelectWorks/HTMLs/0005-02_Pt03_Reflections.html#burke2_1_p34119.

1. Progressive taxes are a good deal

1.   Organization for Economic Cooperation and Development, *Revenue Statistics 1965–2003* (2004).

2.   For married couples in 2006, the standard deduction is $10,300, and the personal exemption is $3,300 per taxpayer and dependent.

3.   For individuals, the Social Security tax is 6.2 percent of wages up to $94,200 in 2006 (adjusted upward each year for wage growth). Employers also pay 6.2 percent on wages, for a total Social Security payroll tax of 12.4 percent on wages up to the cap. The Medicare tax, by contrast, is not capped. It adds another 1.45 percent to both the employee and employer sides of the tax and 2.9 percent to the self-employment tax. Thus, up

to the wage cap, federal payroll taxes total 15.3 percent of earnings, and above the cap, they are 2.9 percent.

4.   The reason the payroll tax is smaller in the bottom-income group than the middle-income group is that a smaller portion of income in this group comes from earned income. There are many retired, elderly people in this group, as well as families receiving government assistance.

2. They're a moral obligation

1.   I gratefully acknowledge the support of the University of Alabama Law School Foundation, the Edward Brett Randolph Fund, and the William H. Sadler Fund. This essay is a condensed version of my most recent article, "An Evaluation of Federal Tax Policy Based on Judeo-Christian Ethics," 26 *Va. T. Rev.* (Winter 2006): 671–764 [hereinafter "Tax Policy and Judeo-Christian Ethics"].

2.   *Matthew* 22:21 "Give to Caesar what is Caesar's and to God what is God's"; *Romans* 13:7 "If you owe taxes, pay taxes."

3.   "Tax Policy and Judeo-Christian Ethics" at 683–87 and notes 26–38.

4.   Ibid. at 690–91 and notes 46–47.

5.   Ibid. at 688–89 and notes 41–45.

6.   Ibid. at 680–82 and notes 18–25; ibid. at 693 and notes 51–52.

7.   Ibid. at 694–95 and notes 53–56.

8.   Ibid. at 695–96 and notes 57–58.

9.   Ibid. at 696–701 and notes 59–67; ibid. at 708–9 and notes 81–82; ibid. at 722–24 and notes 116–22.

10. Ibid. at 701–4 and notes 68–72.

11. Ibid. at 682 and note 25; ibid. at 704 and notes 73–74.

12. Ibid. at 688 and notes 39–40; ibid. at 691–92 and notes 48–50; ibid. at 708 and notes 79–80.

13. Ibid. at 708–10 and notes 79–85.

14. Ibid. at 711–22 and notes 87-115; ibid. at 724–40 and notes 122–59.

15. Ibid. at 741–44 and notes 160–68.

16. Ibid. at 744–52 and notes 169–87.

17. Ibid. at 752–55 and notes 188–95.

18. Ibid. at 756–57 and notes 196–200.

19. Susan Pace Hamill, *A Tale of Two Alabamas*, 58 *Ala. L. Rev.* (2007): 1103, 1131–32.

20. David M. Halbfinger, "Alabama Voters Crush Tax Plan Sought by Governor," *New York Times*, Sept. 10, 2003, p. A14.

21. Hamill, supra note 19 at 1135–38 and Susan Pace Hamill, *The Book That Could Change Alabama*, 56 *Ala. L. Rev.* (2004): 219, 237–38.

22. Adam Cohen, "What Alabama's Low-Tax Mania Can Teach the Rest of the Country," *New York Times*, Oct. 20, 2003, p. A16.

3. They can strengthen the economy

1. Jeff Madrick, "Economic Scene: If Taxes Were Lower, the Economy Would Grow Faster, Right? Economists Say Not Necessarily," *New York Times*, Oct. 31, 2002, p. C2.

2. See, for example, Peter H. Lindert, *Growing Public Social Spending and Economic Growth Since the Eighteenth Century*, (New York: Cambridge, 2004).

3. Thomas Piketty and Emmanuel Saez, "How Progressive Is the U.S. Federal Tax System? A Historical and International Perspective" (National Bureau of Economic Research, working paper 12404, July 2006): 1. Available at: www.nber.org/papers/w12404. Figures from TruthandPolitics.org, "Top U.S. Marginal Income Tax Rates, 1913–2003." Available at: www.truthandpolitics.org/top-rates.php.

4. Calculated based on data obtained from: www.data360.org/dsg.aspx?Data_Set_Group_Id=354.

5. Edward I. Glaeser and Albert Saiz, "The Rise of the Skilled City" (Harvard Institute of Economic Research, discussion paper no. 2025, Harvard University, Cambridge, MA, 2003): 43. Available at: www.economics.harvard.edu/hier/2003papers/HIER2025.pdf.

6. M. Ishaq Nadiri, and Theofanis P. Mamuneas, "The Effects of Public Infrastructure and R&D Capital on the Cost Structure and Performance of U.S. Manufacturing Industries," *Review of Economics and Statistics* 76, no. 1 (1994): 22–37. Available at: www.econ.nyu.edu/user/nadiri/pub81.PDF.

7. Nancy L. Stokey and Sergio Rebelo, "Growth Effects of Flat-Rate Taxes," *Journal of Political Economy* 103, no. 3. (June 1995): 520. Available at: www.jstor.org/cgi-bin/jstor/printpage/00223808/di980614/98p0235u/0.pdf?backcontext=page&dowhat=Acrobat&config=jstor&userID=8cb40b4a@princeton.edu/01cce4405f00501c06186&0.pdf.

8. Joel Slemrod and Jon Bakija, *Taxing Ourselves: A Citizen's Guide to the Debate Over Taxes*, 3rd ed. (Cambridge, MA: MIT Press, 2004).

9. Jeff Madrick, "Economic Scene: If Taxes Were Lower, the Economy Would Grow Faster, Right? Economists Say Not Necessarily," *New York Times*, Oct. 31, 2002, p. C2.

10. Peter H. Lindert, *Growing Public Social Spending and Economic Growth Since the Eighteenth Century* (New York: Cambridge, 2004).

11. Ibid. at 227.

12. Slow growth and higher unemployment rates in Europe are frequently blamed on generous social spending and inflexible labor markets. Some European economists, such as Jean-Paul

Fitoussi, who runs the influential Paris research center *Observatoire Francais des Conjonctures Economique,* argue that high interest rates set by the European Central Bank are much more to blame. Loose monetary policy in the United States, by contrast, sustained by borrowing in China and other markets, is credited with much of the United States' growth and low employment.

13. The argument that publicly financed healthcare systems in Europe produce lower quality care increasingly is absolutely not borne out by evidence. Despite vastly outspending its European counterparts, the United States fares poorly on key indicators such as life span and infant mortality. Quality on advanced procedures has also been found to be mixed. One recent study found that the United States topped the list in survival rates for breast cancer but was at the bottom for kidney transplants. It was typically in the middle in most other areas measured. In 2001, the United States had 2.7 doctors per 1,000 people, compared with a median of 3.1 in the countries in the OECD. France, accused of having a doctor shortage during recent severe summer heat waves, had 3.3 per 1,000.

14. "Growth at Home: The Alarming State of the Job Market, an Interview with James Medoff," *Challenge* 46, no. 5 (Sept./Oct. 2003): 5–14. Available at: www.challengemagazine.com/ Challenge%20interview%20pdfs/Medloff.pdf.

4. Excellent public schools depend on taxes

1. U.S. Supreme Court, *San Antonio School District v. Rodriguez,* 411 U.S. 1 (1973), no. 71–1332.

2. The No Child Left Behind Act is the most recent version of the Elementary and Secondary Education Act, originally passed in

1965. It is an omnibus piece of federal legislation, encompassing the major K–12 federal education programs, including the $12 billion Title I program. Signed into law in 2002, NCLB represents a dramatic and controversial expansion of federal regulation over local schools and districts. The law requires public schools to administer standardized tests in reading and math to every student every year in every grade from grades 3 through 8 and once in high school. Beginning in 2007, it also requires periodic testing in science. NCLB also stipulates a complex system for calculating adequate yearly progress (AYP) for up to ten student demographic groups toward 100 percent proficiency on state tests by 2014. Schools that receive federal funds and do not meet AYP targets are subject to an escalating series of sanctions including provisions for student transfers, supplemental tutoring, more radical "restructuring" or even closure. The law has sparked increasing debate and considerable opposition at the local, state, and national levels. For more information, see: www.rethinkingschools.org/special_reports/bushplan/index.sht ml or www.fairtest.org/nattest/bushtest.html.

3. ACCESS, Overview of School Funding Litigation, available at: www.schoolfunding.info/litigation/litigation.php3.

4. Statement by Paul Trachtenberg of Education Law Center, New Jersey, cited in: John Allen, "Inequality in Funding of Public Education Raises Justice Issues: Quality Often Depends on Where Students Live," *National Catholic Reporter*, May 2, 1997. Available at: http://findarticles.com/p/articles/mi_m1141/is _n26_v33/ai_19389741/pg_1.

5. California Superior Court, John Serrano Jr. et al., *Plaintiffs and Appellants v. Ivy Baker Priest*, as State Treasurer, etc., et al., Defendants and Respondents, Aug. 30, 1971.

6. California Rankings, Education Data Partnership, available at: www.ed-data.k12.ca.us/Articles/calrankings.asp.

7. National Center for Education Statistics.

8. Between 1985 and 2003, the New Jersey Supreme Court issued a series of decisions about school funding equity, beginning with *Abbott v. Burke I* 100 N.J. 269, 495 A.2d 376 (1985). For links to information on all the Abbott decisions, see: www.edlawcenter.org/ELCPublic/AbbottvBurke/AbbottDecisions.htm.

9. *Wiping Out Disadvantages: The Programs and Services Needed to Supplement Regular Education for Poor School Children* (Education Law Center, Oct. 1996).

10. From *Abbott v. Burke II*, quoted in Michael Newman, "Finance System for N.J. Schools Is Struck Down," *Education Week*, June 13, 1990.

11. The Abbott districts in 2005–6, Progress and Challenges, Education Law Center, Spring 2006, and State Survey, Thomas B. Fordham Foundation, available at: www.edexcellence.net/foundation/publication/publication.cfm?id=363&pubsubid=1430#1430.

12. *Rankings of the States 2005* and *Estimates of School Statistics 2006* (National Education Association Research, Nov. 2006).

13. Paul Tractenberg, *Don't Forget the Schools, Fiscal, Budget & Policy Considerations for Tax Reform* (Institute on Law and Education Policy: Rutgers University, March 2006).

14. *Rankings of the States 2005* and *Estimates of School Statistics 2006* (National Education Association Research, Nov. 2006); David S. Cloud, "Record $622 Billion Budget Requested for the Pentagon," *New York Times*, Feb. 3, 2007, p. A11; *Growth and Disparity: A Decade of Public School Construction,* a report

from the BEST (Building Education Success Together) Coalition, Oct. 2006; William J. Mathis, "No Child Left Behind Act: What Will It Cost States?" *Spectrum: The Journal of State Government*, March 2004, p. 8.

6. Pollution taxes may save life on earth

1.   The Congressional Research Service summarized energy tax initiatives taken through 2004 in an issue brief updated on January 10, 2005, entitled "Energy Tax Policy." It found $4.25 billion in tax subsidies on the books for conventional fossil fuels projected for fiscal year 2005.

2.   Renewable Energy Policy Project and Charles Komanoff, as quoted in Public Citizen's "Renewable Energy Is Capable of Meeting Our Energy Needs." See also: www.carbontax.org.

3.   Early in 2007,the House of Representatives voted to reduce recently enacted subsidies for oil and to set aside much of the savings for use later in support of renewable energy, but as of this writing in early 2007, final enactment of these changes remained to be accomplished.

4.   Testimony of Milton Copulos, National Defense Council Foundation president before the Senate Foreign Relations Committee, March 30, 2006. Oak Ridge National Laboratory, (confirming a study done in 1983 by the Congressional Office of Technology Assessment) estimates that waste wood generated by processes like the U.S. Forest Service removal of dead wood and debris to prevent forest fires could be turned into zero-sulfur industrial boiler fuel (such as wood pellets) to produce the equivalent of 5.6 million barrels of oil per day to displace the roughly one-third of our oil that is not used in transportation.

Available at: http://foreign.senate.gov/testimony/2006/
CopulosTestimony060330.pdf, p. 6.

5.   In just one example, members of the "Green Scissors
Campaign," a campaign launched by environmental and other
public interest organizations, identified a range of wasteful
government subsidies of energy and other natural
resource–related industries that in 2003 totaled $58 billion. See:
www.greenscissors.org/energy/index.htm.

6.   "An Assessment of the Available Windy Land Area and the
Wind Energy Potential in the Contiguous United States," Pacific
Northwest Laboratory, U.S. DOE, 1991. The Dakotas, Texas, and
Kansas were among the richest in wind-energy potential. A trunk
line through these states could be tapped into by energy-hungry
markets nationally.

7.   The environmental impact of wind power is nearly always
lower than that of polluting sources, but proper siting and other
precautions are important. Two wind farms are situated where
birds in one case and bats in the other run into them at higher
than expected frequency, though the total for all wind farms is
still hundreds of times fewer than are killed by buildings, house-
cats, cell phone towers, or fossil fuel pollution and fossil fuel-
related habitat destruction alone. Most new farms are planned
for areas where such bird- and bat-kills will be negligible. See:
www.windworks.org and www.awea.org.

8.   Begun in 1992, the production tax credit is adjusted to track
inflation and was by early 2007 at 1.9 cents per Kwh.

9.   "The Department of Energy's Energy Information
Administration has concluded that there isn't much difference
between the cost of electric power plants using wind or traditional

fuels if you take into account a broad array of expenses," according to the *Wall Street Journal*. See "The New Math of Alternative Energy," Feb. 12, 2007, p. R4. One utility has also estimated that the cost of providing electricity through new investments in wind is less expensive than any other source if you consider the "levelized" costs over the next twenty years. See: www.pse.com/energyEnvironment/irpPDFs/June22IRPAG-Final.pdf.

10. U.S. DOE Energy Efficiency and Renewable Energy homepage: www1.eere.energy.gov/solar/news_detail.html?news_id=10675j.

11. See: www.solarbuzz.com/FastFactsUSA.htm.

12. Hydrogen fuel can be produced by using wind power, making it part of an entirely clean energy cycle.

13. Ethanol should be used only as part of a carefully tracked production process that minimizes the impact of cultivation and transport. Using too much ethanol has the potential to impose serious costs by inflating the price of corn for the poor in the developing world, or by encouraging conversion of diverse natural ecosystems, including rainforests, into monoculture farms for the production of such biofuel crops as corn or sugarcane.

14. Other gases include nitrous oxide, tetrafluoromethane, carbon tetrafluoride, hexafluoroethane, and sulfur hexafluoride.

15. EPI study, 1.2.1, available at: www.epinet.org/content.cfm/studies_cleanenergyandjobs.

16. The Kyoto Protocol, not ratified by United States but ratified by most other developed countries, is the binding international agreement under the United Nations Framework Convention on Climate Change that requires reduction of greenhouse gas emissions to 1990 levels by 2012.

17. See "An Integrated Analysis of Policies That Increase

Investments in Advanced Energy-efficient/Low Carbon Technologies," by Donald Hanson and Skip Laitner of Argonne National Laboratory, France, and U.S. EPA Office of Atmospheric Programs, July 1, 2004; its abstract states: "A new analysis by the EPA Office of Atmospheric Programs and the Argonne National Laboratory (ANL), using the All Modular Industry Growth Assessment (AMIGA) system, indicates that a technology-led investment strategy can secure substantial domestic reductions of carbon emissions at a net positive impact on the U.S. economy."

18. Dr. James Barrett, lead author of the 2002 Economic Policy Institute study previously cited, points out that when he did his study, most researchers referred to a tax on carbon rather than on carbon dioxide. The figure of $50 per ton here is a level of tax based on carbon. That carbon becomes part of the greenhouse gas CO_2, or worse, CO, the very poisonous carbon monoxide, if burned with too little oxygen as is too often the case. Some calculate proposals in terms of taxes on CO_2. The difference is a factor of about 3.6. That is, in terms of CO_2, the $50 per ton carbon tax would be about $14 per ton of CO_2.

"In a recent paper, Mr. [Richard] Cooper, [a Harvard economist], suggested an initial tax around $14 per ton of carbon dioxide emitted . . . would raise as much as $80 billion a year in the U.S. . . . . Economists like William D. Nordhaus of Yale and Mr. Cooper of Harvard advocate a tax as the clearest price signal . . . and less susceptible to political tampering and market manipulation than a cap and trade system." See Steve Lohr, "Cost of an Overheated Planet," *New York Times*, Dec. 12, 2006, p. C5.

19. Some activities that result in greenhouse gas (GHG) emissions also have health impacts. Under this proposal these would be

taxed to reflect both health and environmental costs. Air and water pollution and habitat degradation from coal extraction, transport, burning, and ash disposal, for example, cause environmental and health problems and would be taxed at a higher rate than pollutants that contribute primarily to climate change.

20. Low to moderate income defined as being in the bottom 40 percent of the income distribution. We join EPI and others in recognizing that workers and investors in some sectors, such as coal mining, may need to turn to employment in such industries as insulation and wind turbine installation, as is happening in Pennsylvania's new wind energy industry; cheaper imported coal is already starting to displace some U.S. coal and U.S. jobs. Employment offices can make this connection and the Independence Fund could help.

21. Article 3 of the Convention on Biological Diversity and Article XX(b) and (g) of the GATT, as reviewed in the Sea Turtle–Shrimp Appellate Decisions of the WTO, 1991–93.

22. The European Union is considering such border taxes on pollution now. See: www.pointcarbon.com/Home/News/All%20news/EU%20ETS/article18599-467.htm for a November 2006 report describing the plan.

23. The Bush administration promised to propose measures to require constraints on emissions from the developing world when it refused to sign the Kyoto Protocol, which does not require such constraints. Despite suggestions from within the U.S. Agency for International Development (USAID) and elsewhere, the administration failed to follow through.

24. Article 3 of the Convention on Biological Diversity and Article XX(b) and (g) of the GATT, as reviewed in the Sea Turtle–Shrimp Appellate Decisions of the WTO, 1991–93.

25. See: www.panda.org/epo.

26. For links to the full report as well as updates, see: www.hm
-treasury.gov.uk/independent_reviews/stern_review_economics
_climate_change/sternreview_index.cfm.

27. French Prime Minister Dominique de Villepin "also
announced measures to strengthen the polluter-pays principle,
including a 10% increase in taxation of industrial and air
transport pollution as well as waste. Possible other measures
include congestion charges in major cities. A tax on coal
announced in October will also be introduced in 2007." EED
May 10, 2006. Available at: www.endseuropedaily.com/21784.

7. Taxes can promote economic justice for all

1. Survey of Consumer Finances, Federal Reserve Board, 2004.
Available at: www.federalreserve.gov/pubs/oss/oss2/2004/
scf2004home.html.

2. Supreme Court of California, *Lin Sing v. Washburn*, July Term
1862, 20 Cal. 534, 1862 WL 587 (Cal.). The legislative history
summarized in the case notes that these laws were followed in
1862 by an even more explicitly anti-Chinese law, entitled "an
act to protect free white labor against competition with Chinese
coolie labor, and discourage the immigration of the Chinese into
the State of California." This law taxed every Chinese person
over eighteen years of age $2.50 per month during residence in
the state. It was later declared unconstitutional.

3. Meizhu Lui, Barbara Robles, Betsy Leondar-Wright Rose
Brewer, and Rebecca Adamson, *The Color of Wealth: The Story
Behind the U.S. Racial Wealth Divide* (New York: The New Press,
2006), 188.

4. Ibid. at 69.

5. Ibid. at 95.

6. Ibid. at 257.

7. Ibid. at 3.

8. Gerald Prante, "Who Benefits from the Home Mortgage Interest Deduction," Tax Foundation, Feb. 6, 2006.

9. Tom Shapiro, presentation on African American Savings and Wealth Patterns, Center for American Progress, May 13, 2004.

10. Ibid. at 228.

11. Melvin L. Oliver and Thomas M. Shapiro, *Black Wealth, White Wealth: A New Perspective on Racial Inequality* (New York: Routledge, 1997).

12. Mayors Task Force on Poverty, Work and Opportunity (report, Jan. 2007) 19.

13. Michael Paul Williams, "More than Ever, America Needs King," *Richmond Times Dispatch* (Virginia), Jan. 15, 2007.

8. Taxes pay for economic opportunity

1. William H. Gates Sr., guest columnist, "I-920: No, It's a Small Levy, So Help Recycle Investment in the Wealthy," *Seattle Post-Intelligencer,* Oct. 15, 2006. Available at: http://seattlepi .nwsource.com/opinion/288629_noestatetax15.html.

2. Conor Kenny, Chuck Collins, Taylor Lincoln, and Lee Farris, "Spending Millions to Save Billions: The Campaign of the Superwealthy to Kill the Estate Tax," Public Citizen and United for a Fair Economy, April 2006. Available at: www.citizen.org/ documents/EstateTaxFinal.pdf.

3. "Remarks by the President on Veto of Death Tax Elimination Act of 2000," Office of the Press Secretary, The White House, Aug. 31, 2000.

4. Calculation is an extrapolation based on an estimate by the

Congressional Budget Office of the number of estates that could have owed estate taxes in 2000 if a $2 million exemption applied compared to the total number of estates in 2000. See Congressional Budget Office, "Effects of the Federal Estate Tax on Farms and Small Businesses," July 2005; and Internal Revenue Service, "Table 17: Estate Tax Returns as a Percentage of Adult Deaths, Selected Years of Death, 1934–2002," Statistics of Income Tax Statistics, Statistics of Income Bulletin: Historical Tables and Appendix.

5. Joel Friedman and Arloc Sherman, "House to Vote on Permanent Repeal of Estate Tax," Center on Budget and Policy Priorities, April 12, 2005. (Calculation determined by using the Joint Committee on Taxation's estimate of the cost of repeal in 2015 and assuming that the cost of full repeal as a share of GDP would be constant in each year between 2012 and 2021, then estimating the added interest on the national debt incurred as a result of the repeal.) See Center on Public and Policy Priorities, "The Estate Tax: Myths and Realities," Aug. 31, 2005.

6. James M. Poterba and Scott Weisbenner, *The Distributional Burden of Taxing Estates and Unrealized Capital Gains at Death: Rethinking Estate and Gift Taxation*, eds. William G. Gale, James R. Hines Jr., and Joel Slemrod (Washington, DC: Brookings Institution, 2001), as quoted by Ruth Carlitz and Joel Friedman, "Why the Estate Tax Is Not 'Double Taxation,'" Center on Budget and Policy Priorities, June 17, 2005.

7. David Cay Johnston, "Talk of Lost Farms Reflects Muddle of Estate Tax Debate," *New York Times,* April 8, 2001. Congressional Budget Office, "Effects of the Federal Estate Tax on Farms and Small Businesses," July 2005.

8. Center on Budget and Policy Priorities, "The Estate Tax:

Myths and Realities," Aug. 31, 2005, and "Instructions for Form 706, (Rev. Aug. 2003), United States Estate (and Generation-Skipping Transfer) Tax Return," Internal Revenue Service, 2003.

9. John J. Havens and Paul Schervish, "Millionaires and the Millennium: New Estimates of the Forthcoming Wealth Transfer and the Prospects for a Golden Age of Philanthropy," Boston College Social Welfare Research Institute, Oct. 19, 1999. Paul Schervish, "The New Philanthropists," *Boston Globe*, March 3, 2002.

10. A study by the Brookings Institution found that repeal would reduce charitable giving by an estimated $10 billion a year. See Jon M. Bakija and William G. Gale, "Effects of Estate Tax Reform on Charitable Giving," Urban-Brookings Tax Policy Center, *Tax Policy Issues and Options,* no. 6 (July 2003). Declines in bequests by 22 to 37 percent would cost between $3.6 and $6 billion per year, with a reduction in nonbequest donations making up the balance of the $10 billion. A study by the nonpartisan Congressional Budget Office confirmed these findings but estimated the loss of charitable giving to be even higher, at between $13 and $25 billion a year. See David Kamin, "New CBO Study Finds that Estate Tax Repeal Would Substantially Reduce Charitable Giving," Center on Budget and Policy Priorities, Aug. 3, 2004; and "The Estate Tax and Charitable Giving," Congressional Budget Office, July 2004.

11. James L. Huston, *Securing the Fruits of Labor: The American Concept of Wealth Distribution, 1765–1900* (Baton Rouge: University of Louisiana Press, 1998).

12. Larry Mishel, Jared Bernstein, and Sylvia Allegretto, *State of Working America, 2006–2007* (Washington, DC: Economy Policy Institute, 2006): 249.

13. Theodore Roosevelt, *Works* 16: 415, 421. As cited in Sidney Ratner, *Taxation and Democracy in America*, rev. ed. (New York: John Wiley, 1967).

14. Andrew Carnegie, *The Gospel of Wealth* was originally published as "Wealth" in the *North American Review* in 1889. Andrew Carnegie, *The Gospel of Wealth* (Cambridge: Belknap Press of Harvard University Press, 1962): 21.

15. Ibid. at 20.

16. See the "Call to Preserve the Estate Tax," sponsored by Responsible Wealth, www.responsiblewealth.org.

17. David Cay Johnston, "Dozens of Rich Americans Join in Fight to Retain the Estate Tax," *New York Times*, Feb. 14, 2001.

18. Chuck Collins, Scott Klinger, and Mike Lapham, "I Didn't Do It Alone: Society's Contribution to Individual Wealth and Success," United for a Fair Economy, Boston, 2004. See: www .responsiblewealth.org/press/2004/NotAlone_pr.html.

19. William H. Gates Sr., "I-920: No, It's a Small Levy, So Help Recycle Investment in the Wealthy," *Seattle Post-Intelligencer*, Oct. 15, 2006. Available at: http://seattlepi.nwsource.com/ opinion/288629_noestatetax15.html.

20. Peter Barnes, "Capitalism, the Commons and Divine Right" (address to the E. F. Schumacher Society, Oct. 25, 2003).

9. Taxes are good for business

1. "Warren Buffett Talks Business," Center for Public Television, University of North Carolina, Chapel Hill, 1995, as cited in Janet Lowe, *Warren Buffett Speaks: Wit and Wisdom from the World's Greatest Investor* (New York: John Wiley, 1997).

2. The U.S. Chamber of Commerce, for example, notes on its Web page: "Chambers of commerce recognize that the lack of

affordable housing for workers is a significant business concern for area employers—who are unable to recruit and retain entry-level and moderate-wage workers because of their inability to purchase or rent housing near their places of employment." See: www.uschamber.com/icw/strategies/workforce_housing.htm.

3. Stacey Mitchell, *Big-Box Swindle: The True Cost of Mega-Retailers and the Fight for America's Independent Businesses* (Boston: Beacon Press, 2006).

10. Taxes fuel democracy

1. U.S. Supreme Court, *Compania General de Tabacos de Filipinas v. Collector of Internal Revenue*, 275 U.S. 87 (1927), no. 42.

2. Recognition of these threats to democratic institutions prompted the creation in 2000 of Dēmos, a nonpartisan policy and advocacy organization dedicated to promoting electoral participation and civic engagement, a broadly inclusive economy, and a strong public sector capable of advancing the public good.

3. Gore Vidal in the forward to David Donnelly, Janice Fine, and Ellen S. Miller, *Are Eections for Sale?* (Boston: Beacon Press, 2001): ix. Available at: http://books.google.com/books?id-ngegfFnJ1ocC&pg=PR9&1pg=PR9&dq=organized+money+has+long+since+replaced+organized+people+as+the+author+of+our+politics&source=web&ots=L3gqkAZtW7&sig=Bla3QoyaCFQ57U8AS06XJwMYIso#PPR4,M1.

4. Jamin B. Raskin and John Bonifaz, "The Wealth Primary: Campaign Fundraising and the Constitution," Web page of the Center for Responsive Politics. Available at: www.opensecrets.org/pubs/law_wp/wealthindex.htm.

5. For more information on the influence of money in politics

and efforts to reform campaign finance systems, see: www
.demos.org/page464.cfm.

6.   To learn more about barriers to voting and efforts to
overcome them, including Election Day Registration, felon re-
enfranchisement, and implementation of the National Voter
Registration Act, see: www.demos.org/page56.cfm.

7.   The poster child for the problematic exercise of these
incompatible responsibilities is Kenneth Blackwell, the former
secretary of state in Ohio. In the 2006 election, he was
simultaneously the chief election official of the state and the
Republican candidate for governor.

Conclusion

1.   Robert Dreyfuss, "Grover Norquist: 'Field Marshal' of the
Bush Plan," *Nation* (May 14, 2001). Available at: www.thenation
.com/doc/20010514/dreyfuss.

2.   Larry M. Bartels, "Homer Gets a Tax Cut: Inequality and
Public Policy in the American Mind," *Perspectives on Politics* 3,
no. 1 (March 2005): 16. Available at: https://apsanet.org/
imgtest/bartels.pdf.

3.   Jacob S. Hacker and Paul Pierson, "Abandoning the Middle:
The Bush Tax Cuts and the Limits of Democratic Control,"
Perspectives on Politics 3, no. 1 (March 2005): 34, 38.

4.   Robert B. Reich, "Secession of the Successful," *New York
Times Magazine*, Jan. 20, 1991, p. 16.

5.   Jennifer Sloan McCombs and Stephen J. Carroll, "Ultimate
Test: Who Is Accountable for Education if Everybody Fails?" *Rand
Review* (Spring 2005). Available at: www.rand.org/publications/
randreview/issues/spring2005/ulttest.html.

Resources

Americans for a Fair Estate Tax
www.ombwatch.org/estatetax

Americans for a Fair Estate Tax is a broad-based nonpartisan coalition of nonprofit groups, including civil, labor, social justice, faith-based, and environmental organizations, as well as organizations providing human services.

Carbon Tax Center
www.carbontax.org/

The Carbon Tax Center (CTC) gives voice to Americans who believe that taxing emissions of carbon dioxide—the primary greenhouse gas—is imperative to reduce global warming. CTC's mission is to educate and inform policymakers, opinion leaders and the public, including grassroots organizations, about the benefits and critical need for significant, rising, and equitable taxes on the carbon content of fossil fuels.

Center for American Progress
www.americanprogress.org/

The Center for American Progress is a progressive think tank that works to create a long-term, progressive vision for America that policymakers, thought-leaders, and activists can use to shape the national debate and pass laws that make a difference.

Center for Economic and Policy Research
www.cepr.net/

The Center for Economic and Policy Research is an independent nonpartisan think tank that conducts both professional research and public education on the most important economic and social issues that affect people's lives. It is committed to presenting issues in an accurate and understandable manner, so that the public is better prepared to choose among the various policy options.

Center for Popular Economics
www.populareconomics.org/

The Center for Popular Economics is a nonprofit collective of political economists. The Center's programs and publications simplify the economy and put useful economic tools in the hands of people fighting for social and economic justice.

Center on Budget and Policy Priorities
www.cbpp.org

The Center on Budget and Policy Priorities conducts research and analysis to inform public debates over proposed budget and tax policies and to help ensure that the needs of low-income families and individuals are considered in these debates.

Citizens for Tax Justice
www.ctj.org

Citizens for Tax Justice is a nonpartisan, nonprofit research and advocacy organization dedicated to fair taxation at the federal, state, and local levels. Its Web site includes good Web links to state and local fair-tax organizations.

Dēmos
www.demos.org/home.cfm

Dēmos is a nonpartisan public policy research and advocacy organization that focuses on four areas: democracy reform, expanding economic opportunity, restoring trust in a government by-and-for the people, and promoting new ideas in the public debate. Its work combines research with advocacy—melding the commitment to ideas of a think tank with the organizing strategies of an advocacy group.

Economic Policy Institute
www.epinet.org/

Economic Policy Institute is a nonprofit, nonpartisan think tank that provides high-quality research and education to promote a prosperous, fair, and sustainable economy. The Institute stresses real-world analysis and a concern for the living standards of working people and makes its findings accessible to the general public, the media, and policymakers.

Fair Taxes for All
www.fairtaxes4all.org

Fair Taxes for All is a national coalition of over 345 national, state, and local organizations working to defend the progressivity of the federal tax system and ensure that the federal resources are there for schools, healthcare, fire protection, community safety, childcare, and much, much more.

Good Jobs First

www.goodjobsfirst.org/

Good Jobs First is a national policy resource center for grass-roots groups and public officials, promoting corporate and government accountability in economic development and smart growth for working families. Good Jobs First works with a broad spectrum of organizations, providing research, training, and communications and consulting assistance.

Institute for Policy Studies

www.ips-dc.org/

The Institute for Policy Studies is a multi-issue think tank that works to strengthen and link social movements through artic-ulation of root principles and fundamental rights, research and analysis on current events and issues, and connections to policymakers, academics, and activists at all levels.

National Priorities Project

http://nationalpriorities.org/

The National Priorities Project offers citizen and community groups tools and resources to shape federal budget and pol-icy priorities that promote social and economic justice.

Responsible Wealth

www.responsiblewealth.org/

Responsible Wealth is a national network of businesspeople, investors, and affluent Americans who are concerned about deepening economic inequality and are working for wide-spread prosperity. Our three primary areas of work are tax fairness, corporate responsibility, and living wages.

Rethinking Schools
www.rethinkingschools.org/

> Rethinking Schools is a nationally prominent publisher of educational materials, as well as an activist publication, with articles written by and for teachers, parents, and students. Most importantly, it remains firmly committed to equity and to the vision that public education is central to the creation of a humane, caring, multiracial democracy.

The Schwartz Center for Economic Policy Analysis
www.newschool.edu/cepa/

> The Bernard Schwartz Center for Economic Policy Analysis is the economic policy research arm of the New School for Social Research Department of Economics. The activities of the Schwartz Center focus on economic growth, employment, and inequality as they relate to the U.S. economy with an awareness of the global context of U.S. economic developments.

The Sustainable Energy and Economy Network
www.seen.org/

> The Sustainable Energy and Economy Network, a project of the Institute for Policy Studies (Washington, DC) and the Transnational Institute (Amsterdam), works in partnership with citizens groups nationally and globally on environment, human rights, and development issues with a particular focus on energy, climate change, environmental justice, gender equity, and economic issues, particularly as these play out in North/South relations.

Tax Policy Center
www.taxpolicycenter.org

The Tax Policy Center (TPC) is a joint venture of the Urban Institute and Brookings Institution. The Center is comprised of nationally recognized experts in tax, budget, and social policy. TPC provides timely, accessible analysis and facts about tax policy to policymakers, journalists, citizens, and researchers.

United for a Fair Economy
www.faireconomy.org

United for a Fair Economy works to promote fair tax policies at the state and federal level through education, advocacy, media work, and support to local organizing efforts. It publishes a tax-organizing kit.

Urban Institute
www.urban.org/

The Urban Institute is a nonpartisan economic and social policy research organization that analyzes policies, evaluates programs, and informs community development to improve social, civic, and economic well-being. It works in all fifty states and abroad in more than twenty-eight countries, and shares its research findings with policymakers, program administrators, businesses, academics, and the public online and through reports and scholarly books

About the Contributors

John Abrams is co-founder and CEO of South Mountain Company, an employee-owned design-build company on Martha's Vineyard, Massachusetts, and author of the 2005 book *The Company We Keep: Reinventing Small Business for People, Community and Place*.

Chuck Collins is a senior scholar at the Institute for Policy Studies and director of the Program on Inequality and the Common Good. He co-founded United for a Fair Economy and Responsible Wealth. He is co-author, with Bill Gates Sr., of *Wealth and Our Commonwealth: Why America Should Tax Accumulated Fortunes*; with Felice Yeskel, of *Economic Apartheid in America: A Primer on Economic Inequality and Insecurity*; and with Mary Wright, of *The Moral Measure of the Economy*.

Stuart Comstock-Gay is the director of Dēmos's Democracy Program. He was formerly vice president of The New Hampshire Charitable Foundation. Stuart has an extensive record of speaking and writing on issues of democracy, foundation practices, and civil liberties.

John M. Fitzgerald is an attorney with more than thirty years of experience in energy and environmental stewardship and government accountability, for Congress, the executive branch, and nongovernment organizations. In January 2007 (after this chapter was drafted), he became policy director of the Society for Conservation Biology, an association of conservation professionals.

Nancy Folbre is a professor of economics at the University of Massachusetts, Amherst, and a staff economist with the Center for Popular Economics. She is the author of *Valuing Children: Rethinking the Economics of the Family; Family Time: The Social Organization of Care; The Invisible Heart: Economics and Family Values; The Ultimate Field Guide to the U.S. Economy;* and *The War on the Poor: A Defense Manual.* She lives in Montague, Massachusetts.

Matthew Gardner is State Tax Policy Director for the Institute on Taxation and Economic Policy.

Stephanie Greenwood edited this volume while pursuing a master's degree in public affairs and urban and regional planning at Princeton University's Woodrow Wilson School. She was previously a researcher at Good Jobs New York, a nonprofit watchdog and advocacy group that tracks economic development subsidies. Her writing has appeared in *The Nation, Dollars and Sense,* and *Sojourners.*

Susan Pace Hamill has been a professor of law at the University of Alabama since 1994 teaching in the areas of tax law, business organizations, and ethics. In 2002 she completed a master's degree in theological studies at the Beeson Divinity School of Samford University. Her thesis attacking Alabama's state and local tax laws on faith-based moral grounds received national recognition, was named to the 2003 List of Best Ideas by the *New York Times,* and inspired tax reform efforts in Alabama as well as other states. Her latest article criticizes the Bush administration's first-term tax cuts on faith-based grounds.

David Cay Johnston is an investigative journalist for the *New York Times*, currently focusing on taxes. He received the 2001 Pulitzer Prize for Beat Reporting "for his penetrating and enterprising reporting that exposed loopholes and inequities in the U.S. tax code, which was instrumental in bringing about reforms" ("The Pulitzer Prize Citation, 2001," available at: www.pulitzer.org/year/2001/beat-reporting/). He is also author of the book *Perfectly Legal: The Covert Campaign to Rig Our Tax System to Benefit the Super Rich—and Cheat Everybody Else.*

Stan Karp is an editor of *Rethinking Schools* magazine and has co-edited several books, including *Rethinking School Reform: Views from the Classroom*. For thirty years, he taught English and journalism to high school students in Paterson, New Jersey. He is currently director of the Secondary Reform Project for New Jersey's Education Law Center.

Greg LeRoy founded and directs Good Jobs First (www.goodjobsfirst.org), a nonprofit, nonpartisan resource center promoting accountability in economic development and smart growth for working families. He is the author of *The Great American Jobs Scam: Corporate Tax Dodging and the Myth of Job Creation* (San Francisco: Berrett-Koehler, 2005).

Michael Lipsky is currently a senior program director at Dēmos, and a research professor at the Georgetown Public Policy Institute. He was a program officer at the Ford Foundation after serving as a professor of political science at the Massachusetts

Institute of Technology. He is well known in the field of public administration for his classic book, *Street Level Bureaucracy*.

Meizhu Lui is the executive director of United for a Fair Economy, a national nonprofit organization that helps build social movements for greater equality. Her articles have appeared in the *Wealth Inequality Reader*, *Inequality Matters*, and in *Yes!, Orion*, and *Social Policy* magazines, as well as in *Black Commentator*.

Jeff Madrick is editor of *Challenge Magazine*, visiting professor of humanities at The Cooper Union, and director of policy research at the Schwartz Center for Economic Policy Analysis, The New School. He is a regular contributor to *The New York Review of Books*, and a former economics columnist for the *New York Times*. He is the author of several books, including *Taking America*, and *The End of Affluence*, both of which were *New York Times* Notable Books of the Year, and most recently *Why Economies Grow*.

Miles Rapoport is president of Dēmos, and a former legislator and secretary of state for Connecticut. He was a leading expert on electoral reform and fiscal issues as secretary and as a member of the legislative committees on elections and finance. Miles has an extensive record of speaking and writing on issues of democracy, election reform, voter access, and voter disenfranchisement.

Daphne Wysham is a fellow and board member of the Institute for Policy Studies (IPS), founder and co-director of the Sustainable Energy and Economy Network, a project of IPS, and founder and co-host of Earthbeat Radio, which is syndicated in over fifteen states nationwide. Her analysis and critiques have been featured in the the *New York Times*, the *Wall Street Journal*, the *Washington Post*, *The Guardian*, and on BBC, NPR, and Marketplace, among others.

Acknowledgments

I learned a tremendous amount working on this book. I am grateful to each of the contributors for their patience and dedication in putting their chapters together and for the excellent work they do in their own organizations. My thanks also go to The New Press publisher Ellen Adler for her thoughtful encouragement and expertise and to The New Press staff Jyothi Natarajan, Melissa Richards, and Jessica Colter for calm, professional assistance throughout the editing process. Heartfelt appreciation to Avinash Kishore for his generous help with fact checking and tracking down references, and to Benoit Schmutz and Cecile Valadier for timely technical assistance.

I benefited greatly from conversations with classmates and professors at the Woodrow Wilson School. And I drew crucial moral support, good humor, and intellectual stimulation from many friends—especially Rachel and Özsel—from my family, Alice, Bob, Dara, Boris, and David, and from my partner Carl. They all made the year I spent working on this project wonderful.